BIG ENGLISH ⑤

T0345676

Contents

Pearson Education Limited
Edinburgh Gate
Harlow
Essex CM20 2JE
England
and Associated Companies throughout the world.

www.pearsonelt.com/bigenglish

© Pearson Education Limited 2014

Authorised adaptation from the United States edition entitled Big English, 1st Edition, by Mario Herrera and Christopher Sol Cruz. Published by Pearson Education Inc. © 2013 by Pearson Education, Inc.

The right of Mario Herrera and Christopher Sol Cruz to be identified as the authors of this Work have been asserted by them in accordance with the Copyright, Designs and Patents Act 1988.

First published 2014

Eleventh impression 2024

ISBN: 978-1-4479-5088-2

Set in Apex Sans
Editorial and design management by Hyphen S.A.
Printed in Great Britain

Acknowledgements
The publisher would like to thank the following for their contributions:
Tessa Lochowski for the stories and CLILpages.
Sagrario Salaberri for the Phonics pages.

Alamy Images: Irene Abdou 19tl, age fotostock 61, Bubbles Photolibrary 49/6, Mark Conlin 18c, Dennis MacDonald 44/6, Frankie Angel 67/2, Tim Gainey 19bl, GOIMAGES 67/1, 75bl, Hilda DeSanctis 71/3, Ruth Hofshi 18b, Image Source 64 (deckchair, sunglasses), Jonah Calinawan 87/3, Judy Freilicher 11tl, 127, Lana Rastro 12/4, 32c/2, 99b, Iain Masterton 34/5, Mira 2/b, 32t/2, 100t/2, Morgan Lane Photography 22/6, 32b/4, 100t/3, Myrleen Pearson 22/1, 32b/2, 49/4, Neil Setchfield 19br, Simon Price 64 (helmet), Sinibomb Images 22/2, 32b/1, 100b/1, Steve Vidler 41t; **Brand X Pictures:** Burke Triolo Productions 72; **Corbis:** Jami Tarris 18t; **DK Images:** Andy Crawford 68t, Dave King, Andy Crawford 67/4, Susanna Price 15; **Fotolia. com:** 2tun 43l, 64 (bracelet), Aaron Amat 67/3, Africa Studio 64 (balloons), alarsonphoto 34/2, 43r, Artur Synenko 81b/2, asese 4br, Barbara Helgason 34/3, 64 (frame), Beatrice Prève 2/f, bkhphoto 64 (bottle), BVDC 99t, Cybrain 81cr, Darrin Henry 2/d, 32t/3, 128tl, Denis Pepin 77bl, Denys Prykhodov 55tl, 64 (mobile phone), dja65 71/1, 81tr, DM7 60c, Douglas Knight 81cl, EJ White 31bl, emese73 2/c, 81tl, Gelpi 4l, GoodMood Photo 77tl, Haslam Photography 34/4, Herjua 51t, higyou 60t, Igor Klimov 29t, 55tr, 64 (laptop), Jacek Chabraszewski 22/4, JJAVA 86/c, JonMilnes 88t, Kadmy 12/1, 32c/1, kaphotokevm1 12/3, 32c/4, KaYann 76/1, Ken Hurst 31br, 45, 103, Lisa F. Young 11cl, 100b/2, MasterLu 51b, milachka 11tr, 81/3, Milos Tasic 81/4, mirabella 43c, Mitchell Knapton 49/1, 66/2, Monkey Business 2/a, 8r, 44/2, 49/5, percent 77tr, petunyia 70/2, 75br, plutofrosti 55cr, 64 (tablet), 67 (c), Robert Lerich 86/b, Scanrail 73br, 77br, SerrNovik 11bl, Simone van den Berg 22/3, 32b/3, 100b/3, skynet 81b/1, 105, soundsnaps 75 (a), strelov 68b, sumnersgraphicsinc 85, tuja66 75 (b), Tupungato 82; **Getty Images:** Terence Langendoen / The Image Bank 64 (jacket), Uwe Umstsatter 71/4; **Glow Images:**

Aurora Open / Henry Georgi 44/1, Bridge / Jim Cummins / CORBIS 8l, ImageBroker / Ulrich Doering 3, 11br, 32t/4, NordicPhotos / Svenne Nordlov 100b/4, PhotoNonStop / Eurasia Press 41b; **Pearson Education Ltd:** Jon Barlow 31tl; **PhotoDisc:** 83b; **PhotoEdit Inc.:** Jeff Greenberg / PhotoEdit 22/5; **Photoshot Holdings Limited:** C. C. Lockwood 88b; **Reuters:** Borja Suarez 93b; **Rex Features:** David Fisher 20; **Shutterstock.com:** 3Dstock 67 (d), 73tl, 76/4, 78, 83t, 92t, alexnika 71/2, Antonio V. Oquias 86/d, baitong333 44/5, 49/3, bonchan 87/1, Boonsom 76/2, Carlos Caetano 10, 70/4, charles taylor 56, Daniel Padavona 87/4, Ersler Dmitry 67 (a), eurobanks 4tr, 31tr, 63, FERNANDO BLANCO CALZADA 55cl, 64 (MP3 player), 67 (b), fet 2/e, 32t/1, higyou 73tr, HomeStudio 71/4 (Abacus), Imagebroker.net 40, Ivonne Wierink 29b, marekuliasz 34/1, 42, 64 (headphones), marylooo 100t/1, MaszaS 44/4, 128tr, Melanie DeFazio 12/5, Michelle Eadie 93t, Monkey Business Images 1l, Nata-Lia 70/1, Natali Glado 34/6, Natursports 92b, Norman Chan 86/a, Ociacia 66/1, Oleksandr Chub 75 (c), Patrick Breig 36, 60b, PRILL 66/3, Robert Kneschke 12/2, 32c/3, rprongjai 87/2, Rudy Balasko 70/3, 75bc, Renata Sedmakova 76/3, SUSAN LEGGETT 44/3, 49/2, Tomasz Trojanowski 11cr, 37, Wallenrock 19tr, Michael Woodruff 9; **Sozaijiten:** 73bl; **SuperStock:** Fancy Collection 1c, imagebroker. net 1cl, 66/4, Radius 1cr, Stockbroker 1r; **Werner Forman Archive Ltd:** 69b

Cover images: Front: **Shutterstock.com:** Monkey Business Images l; **SuperStock:** Fancy Collection c, imagebroker.net cl, Radius cr, Stockbroker r

All other images © Pearson Education

Illustrated by
Q2A Media Services, Anthony Lewis

Big English Song

From the mountaintops to the bottom of the sea,
From a big blue whale to a baby bumblebee—
If you're big, if you're small, you can have it all,
And you can be anything you want to be!

It's bigger than you. It's bigger than me.
There's so much to do and there's so much to see!
The world is big and beautiful and so are we!
Think big! Dream big! Big English!

So in every land, from the desert to the sea
We can all join hands and be one big family.
If we love, if we care, we can go anywhere!
The world belongs to everyone; it's ours to share.

It's bigger than you. It's bigger than me.
There's so much to do and there's so much to see!
The world is big and beautiful and so are we!
Think big! Dream big! Big English!

It's bigger than you. It's bigger than me.
There's so much to do and there's so much to see!
The world is big and beautiful and waiting for me.
A One, two, three...
Think big! Dream big! Big English!

unit 1 MY INTERESTS

1 Listen. Write the number.

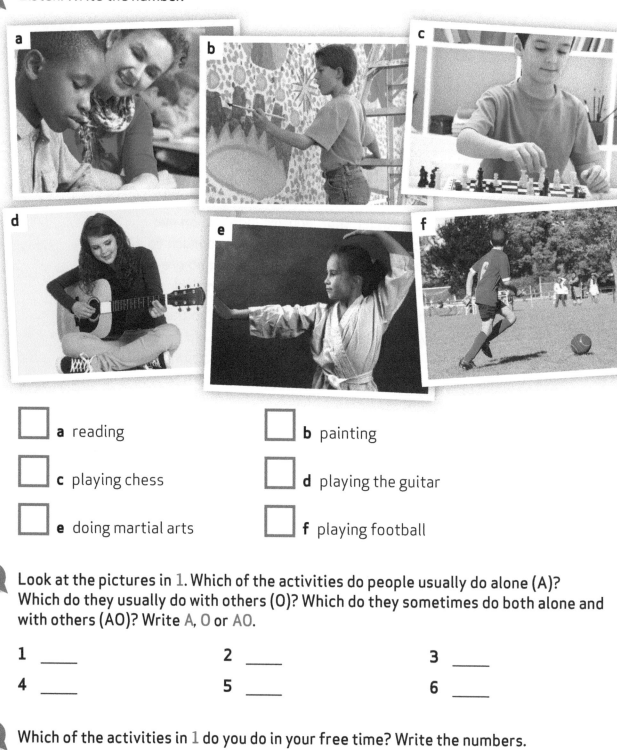

☐ **a** reading

☐ **b** painting

☐ **c** playing chess

☐ **d** playing the guitar

☐ **e** doing martial arts

☐ **f** playing football

2 Look at the pictures in 1. Which of the activities do people usually do alone (A)? Which do they usually do with others (O)? Which do they sometimes do both alone and with others (AO)? Write A, O or AO.

1 ____   2 ____   3 ____

4 ____   5 ____   6 ____

3 Which of the activities in 1 do you do in your free time? Write the numbers.

_____

4 Match the interests to the school groups. Write the letter.

Interests

_____ **1** martial arts

_____ **2** acting

_____ **3** writing articles

_____ **4** playing music

_____ **5** building things

School Groups

a drama club

b science club

c school orchestra

d school newspaper

e tae kwon do club

5 What are you good at? What school group do you want to join? Complete the sentences.

I'm good at _____.

I want to join _____.

What school group could they join?

Susan can move really fast. _____

James is good at taking photos. _____

Elizabeth won a prize for a play she wrote. _____

David's really keen on technology. _____

Anna plays the violin really well. _____

Richard's the best singer in our class. _____

6 Listen and read. Then answer the questions.

Manbury School News Opinion Page

| Home | For Teachers | For Pupils | School Directory | Clubs |

DO WHAT'S RIGHT FOR YOU

bbrown

It's a new school year. Everyone is talking about the new after-school clubs because they're fun. You can learn new things and make new friends. But some pupils aren't interested in joining clubs. They may be shy or scared of groups. These pupils might be good at singing or playing an instrument but they like doing these activities alone. They don't want to join clubs and that's fine.

I'm a shy girl. I enjoy watching sports on TV, painting and playing my guitar. I'm not interested in joining a sports team, art club or the school orchestra. My friends were cross with me because I didn't want to join their clubs so I talked to my mum about it. She said, "It's OK. Be yourself. Do the things you like to do." I want to say to shy children like me, "Do what's right for you. Find friends who are like you. You don't always have to do what everyone else does."

Comments

Silver

I'm shy, too. I always feel bad when my classmates talk about signing up for after-school clubs. I'm glad to know that I'm not the only one.

suki.park

Wow! I love clubs and I never thought some children might not want to join them. Thanks for writing this. Personally, I don't like doing things alone so clubs are good for me.

1 What's this newsletter about?

_____

2 Is the newsletter writer interested in joining clubs? Why/Why not?

_____

3 What does she enjoy doing?

_____

4 Is bbrown shy?

_____

7 What do you think about the newsletter? Write your own comment.

_____

8 Listen. Then read and circle **T** for true or **F** for false.

Cathy: Are you interested in joining a club this year, Ben?

Ben: <u>I don't know</u>… I haven't got much time. I've usually got homework. And when I have got free time, I read my manga comics.

Cathy: Manga? Those Japanese comic books? Cool! Hey, did you hear that there's a manga club at school this year?

Ben: <u>Really?</u>

Cathy: Yes, really! You can sign up in Mr West's room.

Ben: Where did you hear about it? When does it meet?

Cathy: Ken told me about it. I joined yesterday! It meets on Wednesdays and Fridays.

Ben: Oh, good. I can do that. <u>Count me in!</u>

Cathy: <u>Great!</u> See you there tomorrow.

1	Ben's got a lot of free time.	T	F
2	The manga club meets twice a week.	T	F
3	Ben's going to join the manga club.	T	F
4	Cathy hasn't joined the manga club.	T	F

9 Look at **8**. Read the underlined expressions. How can you say them in other words? Match and write the letter.

_____ **1** I don't know.

_____ **2** Really?

_____ **3** Count me in!

_____ **4** Great!

a This is good news.

b I'll be there!

c I can't believe it's true!

d I'm not sure what I want to do.

10 Complete the sentences with the expressions in **9**. Then listen and check your answers.

A: Our class is going to Rome for our class trip.

B: ¹_____! How exciting! When do you leave?

A: Tomorrow morning at 4 a.m.

B: ²_____? That's crazy! How will you wake up that early?

A: ³_____. I hope Mum will wake me up! Hey, why don't you come to the airport with us?

B: Why not? It'll be fun! ⁴_____!

How about **joining** the drama club?	No, thanks. I'm not good at **acting**.
How about **trying out** for the basketball team?	OK. I love **playing** basketball.

11 Look at the pictures of Sue and Kevin. Complete the sentences. Use the correct form of the verbs from the box.

> do tae kwon do   play chess   play football   take photos

1 Sue and Kevin both enjoy _____.

2 Sue enjoys _____. Kevin isn't interested in it.

3 Sue's got a good camera. She likes _____.

4 Kevin enjoys martial arts. He loves _____.

12 Complete the sentences. Circle the correct form of the verbs.

1 A: How about **tries / trying** out for the basketball team?

   B: I'm not sure. I'm not very good at **playing / play** basketball.

2 A: How about **joining / you join** the tae kwon do club?

   B: Great! I love **do / doing** martial arts.

3 A: How about **join / joining** the drama club?

   B: I don't know. I'm not very interested in **acts / acting**.

4 A: How about **goes / going** to the new action film with me on Saturday?

   B: Well, maybe. But I don't really like **watching / watches** action films.

13 Write the questions. Use **How about** and the words from the box.

Do you like playing sports? Yes No
Are you interested in acting? Yes No
Do you like doing maths problems? Yes No
Do you enjoy writing stories? Yes No

Nora

> audition for/school play   join/school news bloggers   join/science club   try out for/athletics team

1 Paul: _____
   Nora: Good idea! I really enjoy playing sports.

2 Paul: _____
   Nora: I don't know. I'm not very good at acting.

3 Paul: _____
   Nora: That's a good idea. I'm good at Maths and I love doing projects.

4 Paul: _____
   Nora: Sounds great! I enjoy writing!

14 Complete the sentences about a friend. Use **he** or **she**.

My friend's name is _____. _____ likes _____ and

_____ 's good at _____. _____ isn't interested in

_____ but _____ and I enjoy _____.

15 Read the questions. Write answers for yourself.

1 How about trying out for the football team?

   _____

2 How about signing up for the book club?

   _____

3 How about joining the science club?

   _____

16 Read. Who likes making lists?

Left Brained or Right Brained?

Tom

"I have a left-brained personality. I'm really good at solving maths problems and I like working alone. I enjoy writing but I'm not good at being creative. I'm very organised. In class, I like listening and taking notes. I usually remember the details when I read. When I study, I write things down and make lists. They help me remember."

Sara

"Honestly, I'm the opposite of Tom. I'm very creative. I love drawing and playing music. I enjoy working in groups and solving problems together. I like surprises but I'm not any good at organising things. Sometimes I talk when I shouldn't and I get distracted when I should be listening. When I study, I draw pictures because it helps me remember."

17 Read 16 again and circle Tom or Sara.

1 Who likes doing projects in groups?	**Tom**	**Sara**
2 Who should be a member of the drama club?	**Tom**	**Sara**
3 Who should be a school news blogger?	**Tom**	**Sara**
4 Who's probably quieter in class?	**Tom**	**Sara**

18 Match the words to the definitions. Write the letter.

_____ **1** personality   **a** good at thinking of new ideas

_____ **2** brain   **b** the unique combination of traits that characterise a person

_____ **3** control   **c** the part of your body that controls how you think, feel and move

_____ **4** instructions   **d** find the answer to a problem

_____ **5** solve   **e** information telling you how to do something

_____ **6** creative   **f** make someone or something do what you want

19 Complete the sentences. Use the words in 18.

1 The _____ has two sides – left and right.

2 Each side of our brain controls different parts of our _____.

3 Can you _____ maths problems easily? You might be left brained.

4 Do you enjoy being _____? Then you might be right brained.

20 Read. What is a 'bunny-hop'?

New Olympic Sport

Do you like riding your bike fast? Did you know that extra-fast bike riding is a sport at the Olympics? Bike racing started as an Olympic sport in Athens in 1896. Over the years, there were road races and track races and mountain-bike racing in the Olympic Games. Then, in the 2008 Beijing Games, a bike sport called BMX became a new Olympic sport. BMX started in California in about 1968. It's a very fast and dangerous sport so competitors have to be fearless to take part!

Both men and women compete in BMX. The bikes are light and very strong. They need to be strong enough for all the jumps and ramps and yet remain light so the riders can travel as fast as possible. The tracks for men are about 450 metres long. They're a little shorter for women. But all the races last only 40 seconds! If you blink, you'll miss them!

The riders have created new words to talk about their sport, such as bunny-hop. A bunny-hop is when a rider's bike goes up in the air. The rider in the picture is bunny-hopping. Another word is 'whoop'. A whoop is a small bump in the road. The next time you ride your bike, watch out for whoops and don't bunny-hop. Stay safe!

21 Read 20 again and rewrite the sentences so that they are true.

1 Only men compete in BMX. _____

2 The bikes are heavy. _____

3 The race lasts 60 seconds. _____

4 A bunny-hop is a small bump in the road. _____

22 Find these numbers in the reading in 20. Write the sentences with these numbers.

1 nineteen sixty-eight

_____

2 four hundred and fifty

_____

3 forty

_____

THINK BIG

Why is BMX dangerous? Do people enjoy doing dangerous sports? Why/Why not?

_____

A good news article includes important information about an event. It includes the answers to these questions: *Who* is the article about? *What* is the article about? *When* did the event happen? *Where* did the event happen? *What happened?*

A good news article also gives other information to make the story interesting but don't forget to answer the questions!

KEY QUESTIONS:
Who?
What?
When?
Where?
What happened?

23 Read the answers (A). Complete the questions (Q) with Who, What, When, Where or What happened.

1 Q: _____? You're all dirty!
   A: I slipped and fell in the mud!

2 Q: _____ does the club meet?
   A: It meets in the science lab.

3 Q: _____'s that over there?
   A: That's my science club leader.

4 Q: _____ does the science club meet?
   A: It meets on Mondays after school.

5 Q: _____ do you do in science club?
   A: We play chess and other fun games.

24 Write a news article. Use the information in the chart. Add interesting information.

Who?	What ?	When?	Where?	What happened?
People who enjoy acting	Audition for the musical *Peter Pan*	Last Monday after school	In the auditorium	More than 20 pupils auditioned
Interesting Information:				
Everyone was nervous. Mr Bannister's going to post the results on the school website.				

THINK BIG

Write Who? What? When? Where? What happened?

Add some interesting information.

_____ It rained.

_____ Played in a concert.

_____ Hampton School orchestra.

_____ At Green Park.

_____ On Saturday morning.

_____

25 Where do these activities <u>usually</u> take place? Write the words in the correct column.

> act on stage   do athletics   play football
> play in an orchestra   play the piano   write articles

Inside	Outside
_____	_____
_____	_____
_____	_____
_____	_____

26 Write questions with how about and the words in brackets.
Then look at the pictures and complete the answers.

1 Peggy: Carla, _____
_____?
    (try out for/basketball team)
Carla: I don't think so! You know I only play
_____.

2 James: Olivia, _____
_____?
    (sign up for/school newspaper)
Olivia: Great idea! I really enjoy
_____.

3 Marco: _____
_____?
    (join/the school orchestra)
Daniel: No, I can't play an instrument but I'm
interested in _____.
Maybe I'll join the drama club.

FAMILY TIES

1 Match the pictures to the sentences. Write the number.

☐ The couple got married.

☐ The family moved to a new house.

☐ The baby was born at 5 a.m.

☐ The student graduated from university.

☐ The family opened a restaurant.

2 Answer the questions about your family. Circle Yes or No.

Last year:

1	Did your family open a shop or restaurant?	Yes	No
2	Did you move to a new home?	Yes	No
3	Did a family member graduate from university or college?	Yes	No
4	Was a new family member born?	Yes	No
5	Did a family member get married?	Yes	No

3 Match and complete the phrases. Write the words.

1 graduated   a _____ to a new place

2 moved   b _____ from business school

3 got   c _____ born

4 opened   d _____ a shop

5 was   e _____ married

4 Listen to the events in Ken's life. Then number the timeline in order and write the events.

TIMELINE OF KEN'S LIFE	
	Age 25 _____
	Age 44 _____
	Age 21 _____
	Age 0 _____
MOVERS	Age 28 _____

THINK BIG

Write the words for these family members. Use aunt, brother, sister or uncle.

My mum's sister is my _____.

My dad's brother is my _____.

My aunt is my dad's _____.

My uncle is my mum's _____.

5 Listen and read. Then answer the questions.

My Amazing Family

My name is Theresa and I have an unusual and amazing family. We're superheroes!
We can do amazing things and we like to help people.

My mum was born in Venice and she moved to Barcelona in 1996. My dad was born
in Barcelona. He met my mum there when they both helped to save people in a house
fire. They got married in 2000 and had three children soon after that. I'm the oldest
child and I've got a younger brother, Tomas, and a baby sister, Tara. Tomas is eight.
I'm stronger than him. I can pick up a car! But Tomas is faster than me. He can run a
kilometre in less than 15 seconds! That's really fast! Tara is incredible! She can make
herself very, very small, sometimes smaller than a peanut. That's why we call her
'Peanut'. I love my family because we're always doing exciting things.

1 Why is this family amazing?

_____

2 Where was Theresa's mum born?

_____

3 Where did Theresa's parents meet?

_____

4 Who's the oldest child in the family?

_____

5 Why does the family call Tara 'Peanut'?

_____

6 Answer the questions.

1 What special power would you like to have? Why?

_____

2 What are you going to do with your special power?

_____

1:27

7 Listen. Then circle the correct answers.

Will: Oh… this is a great picture! What a cute baby!

Deb: Guess who… ?

Will: No! That's not you! Is it?

Deb: Yes… that's me. That's the day I was born.

Will: <u>That's nice.</u> But… what happened?

Deb: <u>What do you mean?</u>

Will: You were so much cuter then!

Deb: <u>Ha ha! Very funny.</u> My mother says I was the cutest baby in the world.

Will: <u>Well, I don't know</u>… . But you were quite cute.

Deb: Thanks.

1 Who's the baby in the picture?

    a someone in Will's family   **b** Deb

2 Will _____ when he says that Deb was cuter when she was a baby.

    a is serious   **b** is joking

3 Deb's mum said that she was the cutest baby in the world. Will _____.

    a agrees   **b** doesn't really agree

8 Look at 7. Read the underlined expressions. How can you say them in other words? Match and write the letters.

_____ **1** That's nice.

_____ **2** What do you mean?

_____ **3** Ha ha! Very funny.

_____ **4** Well, I don't know…

a I don't understand what you're talking about.

b That's not funny.

c I don't think that's exactly true.

d I like it.

9 Circle the correct expressions.

1 A: That's a picture of my brother.

    B: That's nice. / Well, I don't know. You look exactly like him!

    A: Yes, we do because we're twins!

2 A: That's the day we moved.

    B: What do you mean? / Ha ha! Very funny.

    A: We moved from Norwich to Oxford.

    B: I didn't know that!

Language in Action

We **went** to Edinburgh <u>when</u> I **was** eight.
<u>When</u> they **were** children, they **lived** in Manchester.

She **moved** to Cambridge three years <u>ago</u>.
A few months <u>later</u>, she **got** a new job.

10 Find and circle each past tense verb. There are ten verbs.

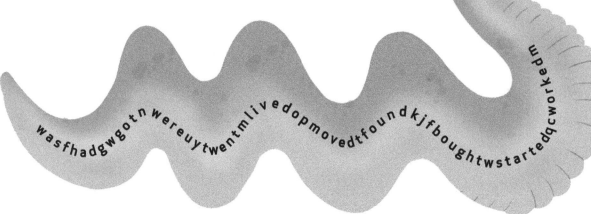

wasfhadgwgotnwereuytwentmlivedopmovedtfoundkjfboughtwstartedqcworkedm

11 Look at 10. Write the past tense form of the verbs.

be	_____	have	_____
buy	_____	live	_____
find	_____	move	_____
get	_____	start	_____
go	_____	work	_____

12 Complete the paragraph. Use the correct form of the verbs in 11.

My mum and dad ¹_____ married when they
²_____ 24. They ³_____ with my
dad's parents because they ⁴_____ to save
money to buy their own house. They both ⁵_____
long hours at their jobs. A few years later, they
⁶_____ a house. That ⁷_____ 15
years ago. They ⁸_____ into the house on my
mum's birthday. I ⁹_____ born a year later!

> Sue's **taller than** Yoko and Mark.
>
> Sue's **the tallest** person in our class.

13 Listen and number the family members.

☐ ☐ ☐ ☐ ☐ ☐ ☐ ☐

14 Look at the picture. Complete the sentences. Use the correct form of the words in brackets.

1 (tall) Joan's _____.

Ben's _____ than Joan.

Ben's _____ child.

2 (young) Maria's _____.

Maria's _____ Joan and Ben. Maria's _____ child.

3 (long) Maria's hair is _____ Ben's hair. Joan's hair is _____ hair of all.

Maria   Joan   Ben

15 Think of a good friend. How are you different? Write sentences. Use the words in the box.

> big   new   old   strong   tall

1 _____

2 _____

3 _____

16 Read. Which dad is lazy?

Good and Bad Dads in the Animal Kingdom

Fathers are important in the animal kingdom. They look after their families and some even look after other families, too. But some fathers are better than others.

The emu dad is a great dad. He finds grass, twigs and leaves. Then he builds a nest for his young all by himself. He then sits on the eggs until the baby chicks are born. During this time he doesn't eat or drink! When the chicks are born, the dad looks after them and teaches them how to find food.

Seahorses do something very special to protect their future offspring. The father seahorse gives birth to his young! He carries the eggs in a special pouch in his stomach for about three weeks until the baby seahorses are born. What an amazing dad!

Lions are fierce predators and can be really scary! A lion dad protects his family and his family can be big. There can be seven lionesses (mother lions) and 20 babies in his family. But he isn't really a great dad. He doesn't often hunt for food. The mums have to do that. The lion dad likes to sleep a lot, especially between branches in trees. He's lazy!

17 Read 16 again and complete the sentences with the words in the box.

> offspring   predator   protect   young

1 A _____ is an animal that eats other animals, like a lion.

2 Some mothers or fathers carry their _____ when they are very young.

3 Male seahorses give birth to their _____.

4 Dads keep their babies safe. They _____ their babies.

What do you think? Are these statements true or false?

THINK BIG

Emu chicks will die if they haven't got a father.   ____ ____

Seahorses carry their eggs in a pouch to protect them from predators.   ____ ____

Lionesses are not good hunters.   ____ ____

18 Read. Who eats Fairy Bread on their birthday?

Special Birthdays

Many cultures around the world celebrate birthdays – in many different ways.

In Nigeria, first, fifth, tenth and fifteenth birthdays are very important. Many parents have big parties for their children and more than 100 people come. They eat a lot – sometimes a whole roasted cow!

A lot of Brazilian children have fun birthdays. Some parents decorate the house with brightly coloured banners and flowers. Brazilians also pull on the ear of the birthday boy or girl. They pull once for each year.

On the first birthday of all Hindu children in India, the parents shave the top of their child's head. When they are older, they have birthday parties. They wear new clothes and give thanks to their parents by touching their parents' feet. At school, the birthday child gives chocolates to classmates.

Australian children have very sweet birthdays! They eat Fairy Bread. This is a slice of bread and butter covered with small sugary sprinkles called *hundreds and thousands*.

19 Read **18** again and answer the questions.

1 What birthdays are important in Nigeria?

_____

2 A Brazilian boy is celebrating his eleventh birthday. How many times do his parents pull his ear?

_____

3 What does a Hindu child do at school on his or her birthday?

_____

4 What are *hundreds and thousands*?

_____

20 Tick (✓) the country with the birthday traditions that you like the best.

☐ Nigeria ☐ Brazil ☐ India ☐ Australia

An autobiography describes the important events in your life and when they happened. The events are in the order they happened. The information often includes:

- when and where you were born
- places you lived
- things you did
- your family and friends
- special memories
- your interests

21 Look at Adele's autobiography. Add events from the chart. Use the correct form of the verbs.

Dates	Events
1988	be born in London, England
1991	start singing
2006	write my first successful songs
2009	win the Grammy Award for Best New Artist
2011	have throat surgery
2009 to the present	start donating to charities

My Life

My name is Adele. My full name is Adele Laurie Blue Adkins. ¹_____

_____ in 1988. I'm an only child. I haven't got any brothers or sisters so my mum and I are very close. I ²_____ in front of my mum's friends when I was only three. I loved music and ³_____ when I was at the BRIT School for Performing Arts and Technology. I was about 18 years old. Three years later, ⁴_____. That was in 2009.

I ⁵_____ but I'm fine now and continue to sing and receive awards for my work. In 2009, I ⁶_____ that help ill children and families of ill children and to charities that help musicians in need.

22 In the Pupil's Book, you were asked to write a story about your life. Now write a different, imaginary story about your life. Complete the chart below and use it to help you write.

Date	Event
_____	_____
_____	_____
_____	_____
_____	_____

23 Complete the sentences. Use the correct form of the verbs in the box.

> be born   buy   get married   move   start

Notes about my family

1 My brother _____ a new car last month. He's very happy.

2 I miss my grandma and grandad. A year ago, they _____ away and now they live in Cornwall.

3 My cousin _____ art school last year. He's a really good artist.

4 I've got a new baby brother. He _____ a few weeks ago. He looks like me!

5 When my parents _____, they were very young. They were a beautiful couple.

24 Complete the sentences. Use when or later and the correct form of the verbs.

When?	Age 16	Age 17	Age 18	Age 19	Age 21
What happened?	learn to drive	get a part-time job	start university	buy first car	graduate

1 Jack _____ to drive _____ he _____ 16.

2 He _____ a part-time job _____ he _____ 17.

3 _____ he _____ 18, he _____ university.

4 One year _____, he _____ his first car.
   He _____ 19.

5 He _____ two years _____ and now he works at a bank.

25 Complete the dialogue. Use the correct form of the words in brackets.

A: Tell me about your family, David.

B: Well, I've got three sisters, Jen, Beth and Kim. Jen is ¹ _____ of the three. (old) Beth is ² _____. (young) And Kim is in the middle.

A: That's nice.

B: Yes. And guess what? Beth is ³ _____ in my family! (tall)

HELPING OTHERS

1 Which activities do you see in the pictures? Write the numbers.

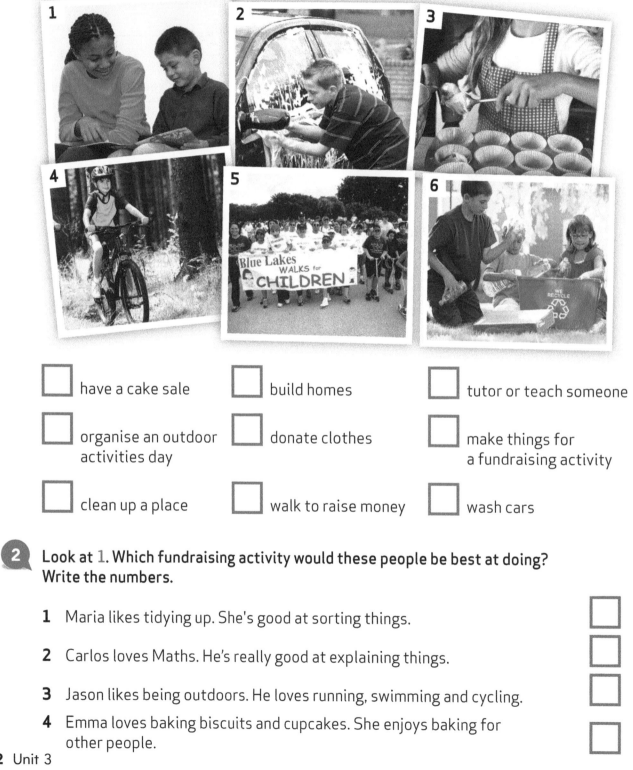

☐ have a cake sale

☐ organise an outdoor activities day

☐ clean up a place

☐ build homes

☐ donate clothes

☐ walk to raise money

☐ tutor or teach someone

☐ make things for a fundraising activity

☐ wash cars

2 Look at 1. Which fundraising activity would these people be best at doing? Write the numbers.

1 Maria likes tidying up. She's good at sorting things. ☐

2 Carlos loves Maths. He's really good at explaining things. ☐

3 Jason likes being outdoors. He loves running, swimming and cycling. ☐

4 Emma loves baking biscuits and cupcakes. She enjoys baking for other people. ☐

3 Unscramble and write the words.

1

rta ifar

_____

2
ekca lesa

_____

3
ehva a tccnoer

_____

4
eakm a diove

_____

5
meak soteprs

_____

6
erwti na riatlce

_____

4 Complete the sentences with the words in 3. Then listen and check your answers.

1 Why don't we have a _____ next week at school? I can make biscuits and you could make a cake.

2 Sara knows how to use the video camera. She can _____ to tell people about our event.

3 We could _____ to make money. A lot of us love to play music.

4 We could _____ and hang them up around school.

5 Let's draw and paint some things and sell them at an _____.

6 Someone could _____ for the school website.

THINK BIG

Year 6 at your school wants to raise money for a local children's hospital. What could they do? How could they tell people about it?

_____

_____

5 Listen and read. Then answer the questions.

On Monday 25th September at 2:30 p.m., Alex in Year 6 wrote…

WE NEED MONEY!

Listen, everyone. As you know, our school needs a lot of things. We need new computers for the computer lab, a new freezer for the kitchen and new chess sets for the chess club. There will soon be some fundraising activities to raise money. Fundraising events are often boring, I know. But I think we could be more creative and do some fun things. I talked to some pupils and here are some of the best ideas:

- Karaoke competition with children and parents. We can sell tickets to each contestant and parents and children can compete against each other.

- Temporary tattoos. We could sell tattoos of cartoon characters and other fun things.

- Pupils vs teachers sports events. I'd love to see this! We could play basketball or table tennis… . Any other suggestions for sports?

- Parents' spelling quiz. Let's have our parents spell words! Could your parent win?

What do you think? Let me know. We can talk to our teachers and see if they like the ideas. Maybe we could come up with a fundraising plan for this year that's really fun! ☺

COMMENTS

arichards
Great ideas! I'll help you! Talk to you later.

carrie_thomas
The karaoke night is a fantastic idea! I know my parents would be interested.

1 What's the blog about?

_____

2 What does the writer think about past fundraising activities?

_____

3 What does the writer think about the fundraising plan for this year?

_____

6 What new fundraising ideas do you have? Add a comment.

_____

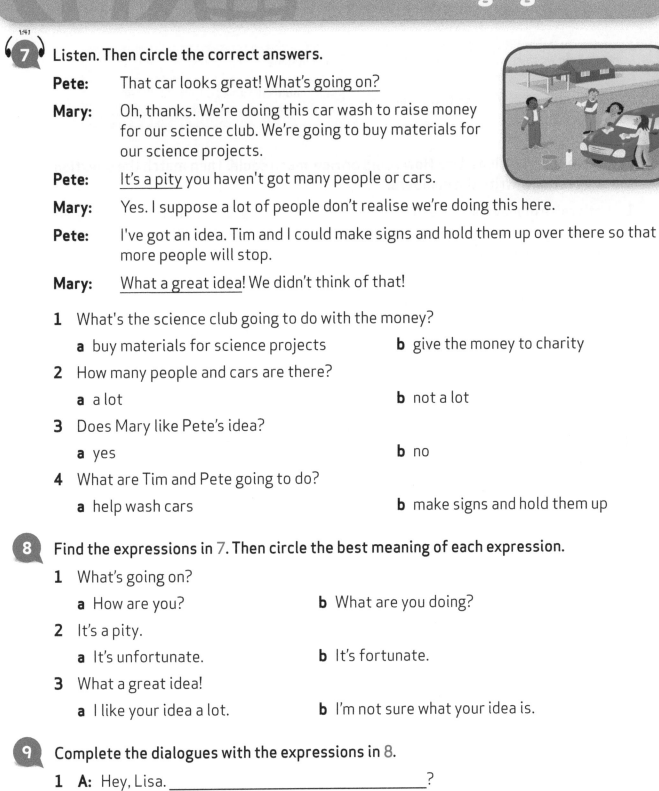

7 Listen. Then circle the correct answers.

Pete: That car looks great! <u>What's going on?</u>

Mary: Oh, thanks. We're doing this car wash to raise money for our science club. We're going to buy materials for our science projects.

Pete: <u>It's a pity</u> you haven't got many people or cars.

Mary: Yes. I suppose a lot of people don't realise we're doing this here.

Pete: I've got an idea. Tim and I could make signs and hold them up over there so that more people will stop.

Mary: <u>What a great idea!</u> We didn't think of that!

1 What's the science club going to do with the money?

   a buy materials for science projects   **b** give the money to charity

2 How many people and cars are there?

   a a lot   **b** not a lot

3 Does Mary like Pete's idea?

   a yes   **b** no

4 What are Tim and Pete going to do?

   a help wash cars   **b** make signs and hold them up

8 Find the expressions in 7. Then circle the best meaning of each expression.

1 What's going on?

   a How are you?   **b** What are you doing?

2 It's a pity.

   a It's unfortunate.   **b** It's fortunate.

3 What a great idea!

   a I like your idea a lot.   **b** I'm not sure what your idea is.

9 Complete the dialogues with the expressions in 8.

1 A: Hey, Lisa. _____?

   B: I'm tidying up. What are you doing?

2 A: I know what we could do to make money. We could sell raffle tickets.

   B: _____. I like it a lot!

3 A: _____ you aren't going to be at the concert tomorrow night.

   B: I know. But I'm really ill. Have a good time without me!

Language in Action

How **could** we raise money for our club?	We **could** have a car wash.
How much **could** they charge to wash one car?	They **could** charge £10 for a small car. For a bigger car, they **could** charge £15.

10 **Complete the questions. Use** How could **or** How much could. **Then match the questions to the suggestions. Write the numbers.**

1 Let's raise money for a class trip.
_____ we raise in two months?

_____ **a** We could write articles about it in the school newspaper.

2 _____ we charge for our winter concert tickets?

_____ **b** We could have a car wash.

3 _____ we tell people about the art fair?

_____ **c** I think we could raise a lot of money.

4 _____ we raise money to buy new football shirts?

_____ **d** We could probably ask for £10 a ticket.

11 **Read the sentences. Complete the sign-up sheet. Write the correct name. Then complete the sentences with** could.

The Art Club Book Sale Sign-Up Sheet

Team 1: Collect books on Monday after school	Team 2: Make posters on Tuesday after school	Team 3: Put up posters on Wednesday morning	Team 4: Sell books on Saturday	Team 5: Tidy up on Saturday at 4:00
1 Jill	1 Gina	1 Carolyn	9:00–11:00: Tanya	1 Sophie
2 Samantha	2 Ben	2 _____	11:00–1:00 _____	2 Josh
3 _____	3 _____		1:00–3:00: Claire	3 _____

1 Anna is free on Saturday at 11:00. She _____.

2 Paul is free after school on Monday. He _____.

3 Sally is free on Tuesday after school. She _____.

4 Mario is free on Saturday at 4:00. He _____.

5 Lisa is free on Wednesday morning. She _____.

12 **Look at** 11. **Think about your school week. How and when could you help?**

_____

How **are you going to** tell people about your cake sale?	We're going to make posters.

13 Complete the sentences. Use am/is/are going to.

Year 6 News

Hi Everyone!

This is a busy week! Our class car wash is this Saturday! We ¹_____ meet in front of the school at 7:30 a.m. Please be on time. Bring a towel and an extra set of clothes – you ²_____ get very wet. I ³_____ bring snacks.

Also, Carol ⁴_____ make posters this Thursday. I hope you can help her. And Jeremy ⁵_____ hand out flyers to parents.

Now we need YOU. Join us! How ⁶_____ we _____ make this a success without you? Can you help? Let me know. I know we ⁷_____ have a great time AND make a lot of money!

See you there!

Mrs Hendricks

14 Look at the pupils' schedule for next week. Complete the questions and answers with am/is/are going to.

CHILDREN HELPING – WEEKLY CALENDAR			
	Me	**Peter and Hugo**	**Sheila**
make a video of the music club	✓		
do a long walk for charity		✓	
sell tickets for the school play			✓

1 A: How _____ you _____ get children interested in joining the music club?

　B: I _____.

2 A: How _____ Peter and Hugo _____ raise money for charity?

　B: They _____.

3 A: What _____ Sheila _____ do next week?

　B: She _____.

Creating an Effective Poster or Advert

15 Match the words to the definitions. Write the letters.

_____ **1** font
_____ **2** images
_____ **3** design
_____ **4** layout
_____ **5** effective

a use of pictures
b the style of the letters
c how the information is organised
d the way the font and images look
e successful

16 Read. What does a successful advert need to have?

Advertisements tell people about a product and make people want to buy it. A successful advert has got interesting design, images and fonts. These things add to the impact of the advert. If the layout is good, the message is more effective.

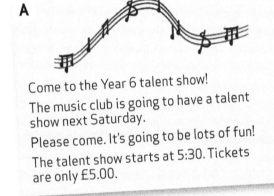

A

Come to the Year 6 talent show!
The music club is going to have a talent show next Saturday.
Please come. It's going to be lots of fun!
The talent show starts at 5:30. Tickets are only £5.00.

B

Come to the Year 6 talent show!

Saturday evening.
Show starts at 5:30.

It's going to be lots of fun!

Tickets are only £5.00.

17 Look at the adverts in 16. Which one is more effective? Tick A or B.

	A	B
1 The font is clear and easy to read.	☐	☐
2 The images don't tell me a lot about the talent show.	☐	☐
3 The layout isn't attractive.	☐	☐
4 The poster's got an interesting design.	☐	☐
5 This poster makes me want to buy a ticket.	☐	☐
6 The information is clear and well organised.	☐	☐

THINK BIG

What do you think? Circle Yes **or** No.

You don't need a lot of skill to make an effective advertisement. **Yes**   No

An effective advertisement can help sell a lot of a product.   **Yes**   No

18 Read. How does Kiva help people?

Companies That **Help** People

Child's Play

Being ill is no fun. Being ill in hospital is terrible! You're alone and you're scared. Your parents aren't there all the time. You haven't got your computer, your video games or any other games. People who worked at video game companies knew this and decided to help children in hospitals. They started a charity called Child's Play.

Child's Play gives laptops, video games and video game consoles to hospitals. They also give toys and books. Ill children can enjoy them and feel a little better. Anyone can give money to Child's Play. It's a wonderful way to help children who are in hospital.

Kiva

Kiva is a company that does what it can to help people. Kiva helps people start their own companies. For example, Josie is good at baking. She wants to start her own business and sell her delicious biscuits and cakes. But it's expensive to start your own business and Josie hasn't got a lot of money. Kiva can help. Kiva finds people to lend Josie money to start her company. When her business becomes successful, she'll give the money back to the people who helped her. People can give any amount of money to Kiva, even really small amounts. It's a great way to help others.

19 Read 18 again and circle the correct answers.

1 Child's Play gives laptops and video games to _____.

   a children at home   **b** children in hospital

2 The people who started Child's Play worked _____.

   a in hospitals   **b** at video game companies

3 Kiva helps people who want to _____.

   a start a company   **b** make biscuits and cakes

4 Kiva helps people find _____.

   a people who will lend a lot of money   **b** people who will lend some money

20 How about you? Answer the question.

You've got £100 to give to charity. Which of the charities in 18 do you want to help? Why?

_____

_____.

A well-written letter is well organised and contains clear ideas. It usually includes:

- the date
- a greeting, such as *Dear Mr Smith,*
- the body of the letter
- a closing, such as *Yours sincerely,* or *Best wishes,*
- your signature (your name)

The letter in this unit offers suggestions. When you write a letter that gives a suggestion, the body of the letter includes:

- your idea or suggestion
- how people can carry out the idea
- why the idea is important

21 Write the parts of the letter.

> body   closing   date   greeting   signature

1 _____ 10ᵗʰ May 2014

2 _____ Dear Mr Green,

3 _____ I think that the school should raise money to help the *Houses for All* charity. This charity builds homes for homeless families. We could raise money for this charity. We could collect coins and raise money that way or we could organise cake sales to raise money.

This project is a good one because all children deserve a good home. We can help. Please think about this idea.

4 _____ Yours sincerely,

5 _____ Teresa Lee

22 Look at 21. Circle the answers in the letter.

What's the suggestion?

How can people carry out the idea?

Why is the idea important?

23 Write a letter to your teacher. Suggest a plan to raise money for a charity.

24 How can these pupils raise money at their school fair? Write suggestions with could.

I'm Maria. I've got a lot of books but I don't need them.

I'm Fred. I'm really good at painting T-shirts.

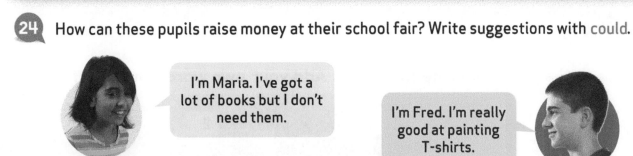

I'm Eric. I've got a video camera and I enjoy making videos.

I'm Gaby. I really enjoy writing.

1 Maria _____ .

2 Fred _____ .

3 Eric _____ .

4 Gaby _____ .

25 Complete the sentences. Use am/is/are going to.

A: How ¹_____ we ²_____ raise money for computers at school?

B: I've got a plan. We ³_____ organise a contest.

A: And how ⁴_____ you ⁵_____ tell people about the contest?

B: I ⁶_____ make big posters and put them up all over school.

A: How ⁷_____ the contest ⁸_____ help raise money?

B: Maybe we could ask pupils to buy a ticket to be in the contest.

A: Well, I don't know.... What kind of contest ⁹_____ you
      ¹⁰_____ have?

B: We ¹¹_____ have an online writing contest. Children can write a
      paragraph titled: *Why we need computers at school.* That's a great idea, isn't it?

A: That's silly! The school doesn't have computers! Children can't write online.

B: Oh. Right.

THINK BIG

1 Look at the pictures. Write the words. Add your own words on the extra line.

MY INTERESTS

1 _____
2 _____
3 _____
4 _____
5 _____

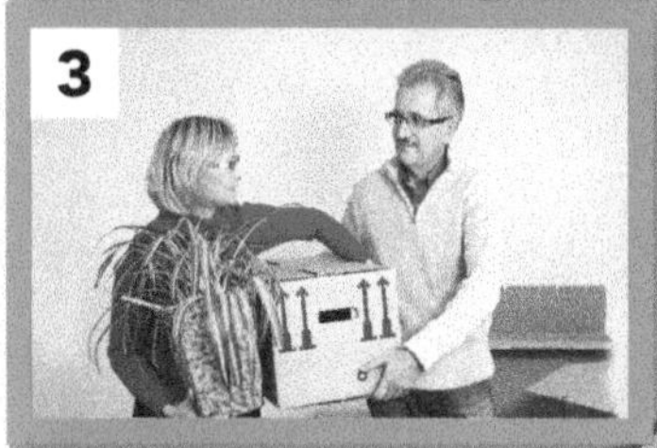

FAMILY TIES

1 _____
2 _____
3 _____
4 _____
5 _____

HELPING OTHERS

1 _____
2 _____
3 _____
4 _____
5 _____

2 Think of a famous person or a cartoon character. Complete the information about him or her.

Name _____	
Interests	He or she is interested in: _____ He or she is good at: _____ He or she likes: _____
Family Ties	Here are some family events in his or her life: _____ _____ _____
Helping Others	Here's a way he or she could help: _____ _____ Here's what he or she is going to do: _____ _____

3 Think about a song your person could like. Use 1 and 2 to help you. Choose a song and write a letter to your person about it. Explain why you chose this song.

SHOPPING AROUND

1 Match the pictures to the places. Write the numbers.

1

2

3

4

5

6

☐ shopping centre   ☐ jewellery shop

☐ craft fair   ☐ shoe shop

☐ electronics shop   ☐ flower shop

2 Where do you like to shop? Tick (✓) your answers.

☐ clothes shop   ☐ video game shop

☐ bookshop   ☐ music shop

☐ flower shop   ☐ jewellery shop

3 Look at 1. Which of these places are there in your neighbourhood? Circle them.

2:04

4 Listen and number the pictures.

5 Where could you buy these presents? Circle the correct answers.

1 a turquoise necklace
   a a craft fair   **b** an electronics shop

2 silver earrings
   a a flower shop   **b** a jewellery shop

3 a beaded bracelet
   a a shopping centre   **b** a music shop

4 balloons
   a a shopping centre   **b** a craft fair

5 roses
   a a bookshop   **b** a flower shop

6 a handmade picture frame
   a a craft fair   **b** a sports shop

Think about some presents for your family.

 THINK BIG

Your sister loves jewellery. What kind of jewellery could you buy her for her birthday?_____

Your mum loves flowers. What kind of flowers could you buy her for Mother's Day? _____

Your dad likes handmade things from craft fairs. What could you buy him for Father's Day? _____

6 Listen and read. Then ✓ the correct person.

▶ Gadgets

▶ Music

▶ Games & Puzzles

▶ Books

▼ Remote control

• Cars and Trucks

• Planes, Helicopters, Boats

• Robots

KIDS RULE:
KIDS TELLING IT LIKE IT IS

Click on any category. Come on, kids! Write a review.

THE RC SUPER SPEEDO RACER
£55.00
Average Rating ★ ★ ★

By Cowgirl (Sydney, Australia)
★ ★ ★ ★

I LOVE this car! It's powerful and runs really well on the wooden floors in my room! It crashes into walls and bounces right off! It's quite expensive but a lot of fun. It's as exciting as the most expensive remote control cars. Actually, I think it's even more fun!

By Tomcat (Canterbury, England)
★ ★

Not great. Not as much fun as the KoolKat Kar. The KoolKat Kar runs very fast on concrete floors and even on carpets. The RC Super Speedo Racer hasn't got a lot of power. It can't even race on carpets. The RC Super Speedo Racer is less expensive but for a few pounds more you can get the KoolKat Kar and have a lot more fun!

	Cowgirl	Tomcat
1 Who likes the RC Super Speedo Racer?	☐	☐
2 Who thinks the RC Super Speedo Racer isn't powerful?	☐	☐
3 Who thinks the RC Super Speedo Racer is less exciting than the more expensive remote cars?	☐	☐
4 Who thinks the RC Super Speedo Racer is expensive?	☐	☐
5 Who likes racing powerful cars that can race on carpets?	☐	☐

7 Answer the question.

Which car would you like to buy: The RC Super Speedo Racer or the KoolKat Kar? Why?

2:09

8 Listen. Then answer the questions.

Jen: <u>How about</u> this one? It got some really great reviews. Look.

Eddie: <u>Oh, yes?</u> Is it as nice as yours?

Jen: <u>Definitely.</u> It's a really good player and it's the least expensive one in the shop.

Eddie: <u>Yeah, but</u> it's £85! I haven't got that much money.

Jen: Yes, but look. It's on sale! Let's see, it's only £60. It's got four gigabytes of memory. And it comes with a free case.

Eddie: Wow! I really like the design, too. It's perfect! There's only one problem.

Jen: What?

Eddie: It's already sold out.

Jen: <u>You're joking!</u>

1 Who knows more about mp3 players, Jen or Eddie? _____

2 Does Eddie need to buy a case for the mp3 player? _____

3 Why doesn't Eddie buy the mp3 player? _____

9 Look at 8. Read the underlined expressions. How can you say them in other words? Match and write the letter.

_____ 1 How about…?   **a** I'm really disappointed!

_____ 2 Oh, yes?   **b** I know but…

_____ 3 Definitely.   **c** What do you think of…?

_____ 4 Yeah, but   **d** Really?

_____ 5 You're joking!   **e** Yes.

10 Complete the dialogue with the expressions in 9.

A: ¹_____ going to the craft fair? There's a big one today.

B: ²_____ Where is it?

A: It's in the park, near school.

B: Great. Maybe I can get a birthday present for my brother.

A: ³_____

B: Hey, did you feel that? It's raining!

A: ⁴_____ Now we can't go!

Language in Action

The blue shoes are **expensive**. The red shoes are **more expensive than** the blue shoes. The black shoes are **the most expensive** of all. The red shoes are not **as expensive as** the black shoes.	The white shoes are **less expensive than** the blue shoes. The white shoes are **the least expensive** of all.

11 Look at the ratings. Circle the correct answers.

Film Reviews
Category: Sci Fi

The Story	Horrible ★	Boring ★ ★	OK ★ ★ ★	Interesting ★ ★ ★ ★	Amazing ★ ★ ★ ★ ★
The Acting	Terrible ★	Disappointing ★ ★	OK ★ ★ ★	Very Good ★ ★ ★ ★	Extraordinary ★ ★ ★ ★ ★
Popularity	Flop ★	Not Popular ★ ★	OK ★ ★ ★	Very Popular ★ ★ ★ ★	Extremely Popular ★ ★ ★ ★ ★

	Story	Acting	Popularity
Robots of the Universe	★ ★ ★ ★ ★	★ ★	★ ★ ★ ★
Princess of Evil	★ ★ ★ ★	★ ★ ★	★ ★ ★ ★ ★
The Pirates	★	★ ★ ★ ★ ★	★ ★ ★

1 *The Pirates* is **less / more** popular than *Princess of Evil*.

2 The story of *Princess of Evil* is **less / more** interesting than the story of *The Pirates*.

3 The acting in *Princess of Evil* is **less / more** extraordinary than the acting in *Robots of the Universe*.

4 *The Pirates* is **the most / the least** popular film.

5 The story of *Robots of the Universe* is **the least / the most** amazing.

6 *Princess of Evil* is **the most / the least** popular film.

12 Look at the ratings in 11. Then complete the sentences with more/less ... than or the most/the least.

1 The story of *Robots of the Universe* is _____ amazing _____ the story of *Princess of Evil*.

2 The acting in *Robots of the Universe* is _____ extraordinary of all the films.

3 The story in *The Pirates* is _____ boring of all.

4 The story in *The Pirates* is _____ interesting _____ the story in the other two films.

13 Complete the sentences. Use **as … as** or **not as … as** and the words in brackets.

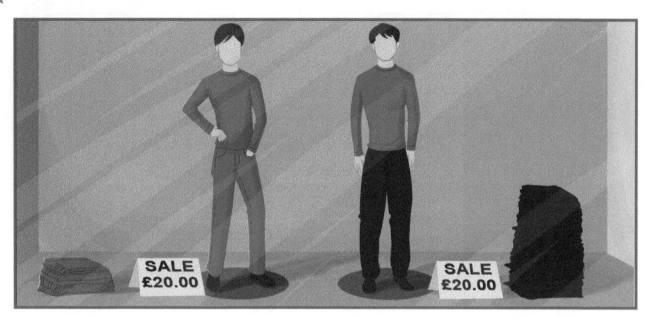

1 The black jeans are _____ the blue jeans. (fashionable)

2 The black jeans are _____ the blue jeans. (cheap)

3 The blue jeans are _____ the black jeans. (baggy)

4 The black jeans are _____ the blue jeans. (popular)

5 The blue jeans are _____ the black jeans. (comfortable)

The price of those trainers is **too** high.	The price isn't low **enough**.
Those jeans are **too** baggy.	The jeans aren't tight **enough**.

14 Look at **13**. Circle the correct answers.

1 My brother wears really baggy jeans. The blue jeans _____ for him.

   a aren't baggy enough   **b** are too baggy

2 I like colourful trousers. Those jeans _____ for me.

   a aren't colourful enough   **b** are too colourful

3 I usually wear white jumpers with my jeans. That jumper _____ for me.

   a isn't bright enough   **b** is too bright

4 We never buy jeans that are too expensive. These jeans are perfect.
The price _____.

   a is cheap enough   **b** is too cheap

15 Complete the puzzle with the words in the box.

coins
livestock
metal
paper
shells
trade

ACROSS

3 Exchange one thing for another

6 Cows and goats

7 Round metal money

DOWN

1 Bank notes are made of this.

2 This is very shiny – silver is one type of this.

4 Some animals live in these.

16 Read. Who used the first paper money?

The Idea for Paper Money

The story of paper money is a fascinating one. The use of bank notes started in the Tang Dynasty. The Tang Dynasty existed in China from 618–907.

Before Chinese people used paper money, they used coins. The coins were round and had a square hole in the middle. They kept their coins on a rope so the more coins they had on the rope, the heavier the rope would be. Rich people found that their ropes of coins were too heavy to carry around easily. So what did they do? They left their strings of coins with someone they trusted and that person gave them a piece of paper with a note saying the amount of money he was keeping for them. When the rich man wanted his money, he took the paper to that trusted person and he got his coins back. This was a good idea, don't you think?

17 Read 16 again and answer the questions. Use short answers.

1 How did Chinese people keep money long ago?

_____

2 What did rich people do with their coin ropes when they were too heavy?

_____

3 What did that trusted person give the coin owner?

_____

18 Read. Why is bargaining a good skill in some places?

SHOPPING IS FUN!

How to shop in Chatuchak Market, Bangkok

Chatuchak Market is a great place to bargain. Everyone bargains here. When you bargain, you try to pay a lower price for something. Here's an example. You want to buy a hat. The hat costs £20. You say to the vendor, the person who sells the hat, "I want to pay £10." The vendor says, "That's too cheap. How about £15?" You say, "Definitely not! That's still too expensive. How about £12?" The vendor says, "OK, £12." Because you bargained, you just paid £8 less for the hat!

Bargaining is a good skill to have when you shop in some places. You can buy things for less money and this means you can buy more things.

Mandarake in Akihabara, Tokyo

The most popular place in Akihabara could be Mandarake. This is the largest manga and anime shop in the world. The shop includes all eight floors in a building. It's full of DVDs of anime films, comic books and action figures of your favourite characters. The customers who shop at Akihabara are very interesting, too. Some of them dress up to look like the characters in animation films, like Sailor Moon, Pokemon and Super Mario. These people wear costumes and make-up and really enjoy acting like their favourite characters.

19 Read **18** again and circle **T** for true or **F** for false.

1 You can bargain at Chatuchak Market.	**T**	**F**
2 When you bargain, you want to pay more for something.	**T**	**F**
3 Mandarake is the largest manga and anime shop in the world.	**T**	**F**
4 Some customers at Mandarake dress up like sports heroes.	**T**	**F**

THINK BIG

Circle and write.

I **want to / don't want to** go to Chatuchak Market because

_____ .

I **want to / don't want to** go to Akihabara because

_____ .

A good product review describes what is good and bad about a product and gives a recommendation. A recommendation tells the readers if they should buy the product.

Here are ways to say if a product is good or bad:

Good

It's the best.
They're worth the money.
It's great.

Bad

It's terrible.
They're not worth the money.
It isn't great.

Here are ways to give a recommendation:

I definitely recommend this product.
This product isn't great but [say why some people might like it].
I don't recommend this product because…

Remember to explain your ideas.

20 **Read the product review. Answer the questions. Write the sentence numbers.**

¹I bought my Wrap-Arounds at Cheap Charlie. ²They aren't great headphones, but they're good for people who haven't got a lot of money. ³You can buy more expensive headphones and get more amazing sound, but why? ⁴I think they're worth the money, especially if you don't need to hear extraordinary sound. ⁵I recommend Wrap-Arounds because they offer good sound for little money.

Which sentence explains…

1 who would like the headphones?

2 why the headphones are worth the money?

3 if you should buy the headphones?

21 **Choose a gadget you have got or want. Write a review.**

_____

_____

_____

_____

_____

─ TIPS ─

To write a good review you need to decide these things:

1 Do you like the product or not? Why/Why not?

2 What's good or bad about it?

3 Is it worth the money?

4 Will you recommend it or not?

22 Write the words in the correct column.

> bracelet   clothes shop   craft fair   digital camera   earrings
> flower shop   headphones   mp3 player   necklace

Jewellery	Gadgets	Places
_____	_____	_____
_____	_____	_____
_____	_____	_____

23 Look at the ratings. Complete the sentences. Write more/less popular than and the most/the least popular.

★★★★★   ★★★   ★★★★

1 The turquoise necklace is _____ the beaded bracelet.

2 The beaded bracelet is _____ the silver earrings.

3 The turquoise necklace is _____ of them all.

4 The beaded bracelet is _____ of them all.

24 Write the sentences. Use too or not ... enough and the words in brackets.

1 These shoes look like boats on my feet. They're _____. (big)

2 This digital camera costs a lot of money. It's _____. (expensive)

3 I can't hear the video. It's _____. (loud)

4 These headphones always break. They're _____ (strong).

HOLIDAY TIME

1 Which holidays do you see in the pictures? Write the numbers.

☐ riding a bike in the forest

☐ snorkelling on a coral reef

☐ lying on the beach

☐ hiking in the mountains

☐ kayaking down a river

☐ skiing in the snow

☐ doing water sports on a lake

☐ visiting an amusement park

2 Look at 1. Which holiday would you like the best? Which holiday would you like the least? Rank the holidays and write their numbers in the chart.

The least 👍	👍👍	👍👍👍	👍👍👍👍	The most 👍👍👍👍👍

3 Write the words in the correct rows.

| an anorak | a helmet | insect repellent | a life jacket | a map |
| sunglasses | sunscreen | a water bottle | a warm jacket | |

useful clothing	
useful for eyes	
useful for skin	
useful for safety/health	

4 Look at 3. Complete the sentences.

1 I'm wearing _____ because there are a lot of insects in the woods.

2 Take _____. You'll get thirsty on the hike.

3 When you go horse riding, wear _____. You could fall.

4 I'm glad we took _____ on our bike trip. We almost got lost.

5 It was very cold in the mountains so I wore _____.

6 The captain of the boat gave me _____ because the water was rough and dangerous.

7 I didn't put on enough _____ at the beach and now I've got sunburn.

8 When you walk on the beach in winter, it can be windy and wet. Be sure to wear _____.

I'm going to go biking on a forest path on a very sunny day.
It's sometimes windy in the afternoons.
What should I take to be comfortable and safe?

THINK BIG

_____, _____, _____,

_____, _____

_____ and _____

5 Listen and read. Then answer the questions.

A Family's Kayaking Trip

Joe felt awful when he woke up. His head hurt. His stomach hurt. His ears hurt. He was sad because his family was going kayaking soon. His mum looked at him and said, "Sorry, Joe, you're too ill to go with us. You're going to stay at home with Grandma." Joe was cross! It wasn't fair!

His family said goodbye and left. Joe was staring at the TV when his grandma came in. She said, "Don't worry, Joe. You'll go kayaking another day."

Joe stared at the ceiling. He was thinking about his family. They were probably having a wonderful time. He closed his eyes and pictured them. They were in their kayaks on the river, laughing and having fun. There were deer and rabbits on the river banks and birds everywhere.

He was sleeping when his family returned. He woke up as they came into his room. They looked miserable. His mum said, "We had a terrible time. We all got mosquito bites. I fell and hurt my arm on the way to the river. Your sister fell into the river when she got out of her kayak. Your dad hit his head on a tree branch hanging over the river. You're very lucky that you stayed at home."

1 What did Joe's family do?

_____

2 Why didn't Joe go with his family?

_____

3 How did Joe imagine his family's day?

_____

4 Why was Joe surprised when he saw his family?

_____

6 Answer the questions. Explain your answers.

1 Do you think Joe still wants to go kayaking?

_____

2 Do you think his family wants to go kayaking again?

_____

3 Do you want to go kayaking?

_____

2:21

7 Listen. Then circle the correct answers.

Eve: So <u>how did your holiday go?</u>

Gina: It was terrible. On the second day, we went shopping in a small town. I was quite excited at first. One shop had lovely souvenirs. You know, T-shirts and magnets, <u>stuff like that</u>.

Eve: <u>I bet</u> you got something wonderful.

Gina: Well, I <u>had my eye on</u> a really beautiful pair of earrings. But while I was shopping, I lost my purse. By the time I found it, all the shops were closed!

Eve: Aw, that's <u>a shame</u>. But I suppose you saved a lot of money that way!

Gina: Ha ha! Very funny!

1 Did Gina have a good time?

   a Yes, she did.

   b No, she didn't.

2 Did Gina really think Eve was funny?

   a Yes, she did.

   b No, she didn't.

8 Look at 7. Read the underlined expressions. Think about the meaning. Then circle the correct answers.

1 Eve asks, "How did your holiday go?" What does she want to know?

   a how Gina travelled while on holiday

   b whether Gina enjoyed her holiday

2 What other "stuff like that" can you buy at a souvenir shop?

   a postcards, tourist books and maps

   b cookers, fridges and desks

3 What does Eve mean when she says, "I bet"?

   a I think.

   b I know.

4 Gina "had her eye on" a pair of earrings. What did she want to do?

   a She wanted to buy them.

   b She looked at them closely.

5 When Eve says, "a shame", what does she mean?

   a I'm sorry you didn't feel well.

   b I'm sorry the shops were closed.

9 Complete the dialogue with the expressions in 8.

A: Last week, I went to a great street market in Corsica. I ¹_____ some beautiful scarves there. ²_____ you'd like them. They were your favourite colours.

B: What else did they have?

A: Local food and sweets, traditional pottery… ³_____. It was all amazing!

| What **was** he **doing** when he got hurt? | He **was riding** a horse when he got hurt. |
| What happened while they **were hiking**? | They got lost while they **were hiking**. |

10 Find and circle the four verbs in the iguana's tail. Use the verbs to answer the question.

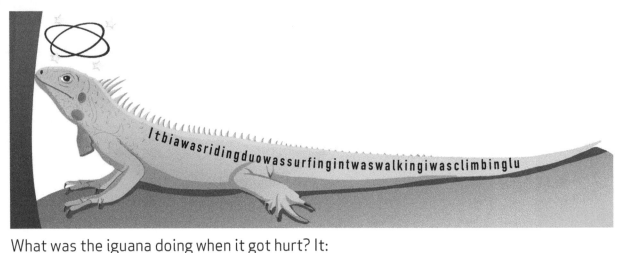

What was the iguana doing when it got hurt? It:

1 _____
2 _____
3 _____
4 _____

11 Match the two parts of the sentences. Write the letters.

_____ **1** While Jack was hiking in the snowy mountains, ...

_____ **2** Sue and Ben sang songs...

_____ **3** Steve was riding his bicycle...

_____ **4** When Jim and his mum were driving to the airport, ...

a he got lost and very cold.

b when he rode into a tree.

c they realised they didn't have the plane tickets!

d while they were kayaking down the river.

12 Look at 11. Answer the questions.

1 What was Jack doing when he got lost in the mountains? _____

_____

2 What happened while Sue and Ben were singing? _____

_____

3 What was Steve doing when he hit a tree? _____

_____

Was he riding his bike when it started to rain?	Yes, he was./No, he wasn't.
Were you swimming when you got sunburnt?	Yes, I was./No, I wasn't.

13 Complete the questions with the correct form of wear. Then write the answers.

1 _____ sunglasses when you saw him on the beach?

_____

2 _____ life jackets when they got splashed by a wave?

_____

3 _____ a warm jacket when she climbed up Greenfell Mountain?

_____

4 _____ insect repellent when you saw her?

_____

5 _____ a helmet when he fell off his bike?

_____

6 _____ sunscreen when you saw her at the beach?

_____

14 Read. What was Jim's problem?

Jim's Problem

Jim was lying on the beach when he realised he was sunburnt. He was also hungry and thirsty. So he went to Beach Shack. He wanted to buy some things. He picked up three bags of crisps, a bottle of water and some sunscreen. But while Jim was adding up the cost, he realised he had a problem. He didn't have enough money! He could solve his problem but he had to make some choices. He had to put back two bags of crisps.

Oh, no! I've only got £9.33!

BEACH SHACK

CRISPS	£1.09
WATER	£1.25
SUNSCREEN	£6.99

15 Read 14 again and circle the correct answers.

1 How much more money did Jim need?

 a £11.51 **b** £2.18

2 How did Jim solve his problem?

 a He bought one bag of crisps. **b** He bought a bottle of water.

3 How many items did Jim buy?

 a He bought five items. **b** He bought three items.

4 What maths did Jim use to find the totals?

 a addition only **b** addition and multiplication

16 How about you? How would you solve the problem?

_____

_____

_____

_____

_____

_____

_____

_____

17 Read. What is a 'staycation'?

A Staycation in Italy

Holidays are wonderful times to be with family and explore new places and cultures. Sometimes families like to stay at home. They don't like to travel but they do like to explore new places and cultures. How can they do both? These families can go on a 'staycation'.

Here is how a staycation works. Your family decides on a culture and country that they want to know more about. They do research and find out about that culture's music, crafts, food, art and other things. Then they try to create the culture in their home during the holiday.

For example, say that your family wants to learn more about Italian culture. Your family would do research and find out the following things:

- popular Italian food
- popular Italian music
- popular Italian stories
- Italian art
- Italian holidays and other events
- the Italian language

During the staycation, your family would plan activities to do together to learn about Italian culture. You might eat at Italian restaurants, study Italian artists at a museum and see Italian films.

Staycations are a great way to enjoy your family, stay at home and learn about the world, too!

18 Read 17 again and circle T for true or F for false.

On a staycation, families:

1	stay at homes around the world.	T	F
2	learn about interesting places and cultures from home.	T	F
3	are not interested in other places and cultures.	T	F
4	learn together.	T	F

Imagine your family is going on a staycation. What culture would you like to learn about?

_____

What are two things you would like to learn about that culture?

_____

_____

Writing postcards is a great way to share your holiday with friends and family. Choose a postcard with a picture of a place you visited or plan on visiting. On the other side, there is a space for the address of the person you are writing to and a space for a short note about the picture or your trip. A postcard includes in this order:

- the **date** (5ᵗʰ July)
- a **greeting** (Hi or Dear …)
- a **body** with information about the place or your plans (I'm having a great time! We went to the beach yesterday.)
- a **closing** (See you soon! or I miss you!)

Don't forget to sign your name. You want your friends and family to know the postcard comes from you! And on the right side of the card, don't forget to put the full address of the person you are writing to (name, street address, town/city, postcode, country).

19 **Write the parts of the postcard.**

1 _____ See you soon!

2 _____ Dear Aunt Edna,

3 _____ 22ⁿᵈ August

4 _____ I'm so happy. I'm having a wonderful time with my family in South Africa. The weather's warm. The animals in the safari park were amazing. Tomorrow we're going to Cape Town.

20 **Imagine you are visiting a place you know well. Answer these questions.**

What's the name of the place? _____

What are you doing there? _____

What exciting things have you seen? _____

Are you enjoying yourself? Why/Why not? _____

What's your teacher's address at school? _____

21 **Use your answers in 20. Write a postcard to your teacher about that place.**

Which is the odd one out? Why?

letter / postcard / email

_____

22 Find and circle the words. Then write the words in the correct columns.

> biking   campsite   helmet   rafting   skiing   tent

c	s	d	x	d	g	d	v	m	c
r	a	f	t	i	n	g	r	e	k
n	g	m	t	f	a	s	g	k	u
g	o	t	p	l	k	i	n	g	n
e	b	l	o	s	k	i	i	n	g
u	i	g	t	u	i	g	l	d	i
l	k	o	i	f	g	t	e	n	t
t	i	i	h	e	l	m	e	t	g
o	n	w	r	i	t	i	n	g	a
n	g	a	e	n	t	t	g	i	t
r	c	f	o	i	a	s	f	n	o

Holiday activities

_____

_____

_____

Holiday things

_____

_____

_____

23 Complete the sentences. Use the correct form of the words from the box.

> driving   looking   putting on   reading

1 We _____ to the amusement park when it started to rain.

2 My dad _____ at a map when he saw the snake right in front of him!

3 My mum got sunburnt while she _____ her book on the beach.

4 I _____ sunscreen when I got stung by a bee.

24 Read. Then answer the questions.

> Yesterday morning, Tim and Jill were swimming in the lake. Yesterday afternoon, Jill went hiking while Tim was at a picnic.

1 Was Tim hiking yesterday morning?

_____

2 Was Jill hiking yesterday afternoon?

_____

3 Were Tim and Jill swimming in the lake yesterday?

_____

unit 6 THE FUTURE

1 Which of these inventions do you think will be common in shops by 2020? Tick (✓) your answers.

1. 3D video games on sale! Be in the game!
2. Spend your next family holiday on the moon! Book your next trip on the Moon Cruiser.
3. Buzz Around on Super Highways! Buy the new Fly Car.
4. Chameleon Clothes! Clothes that Change Colours! Buy now and save!
5. Live in a Smartie House with Robot Help! Never tidy up again!

- ☐ 3D video games
- ☐ Moon Cruiser
- ☐ Fly Car
- ☐ Chameleon Clothes
- ☐ Robot Help

2 Look at 1. Which inventions would you like to buy? Circle the numbers.

1   2   3   4   5

3 What can you do with these electronic devices? Tick (✓) your answers.

You can...				
	smartphone	mp3 player	tablet	laptop computer
1 Make phone calls				
2 Write essays and do homework				
3 Listen to music				
4 Watch films and play games				
5 Text people				

4 Unscramble the words. Use the words in 3.

1 She listens to music on her _____. 3pm lpyrae

2 They read stories on their _____. ptmsrahneo

3 He watches films on his _____. taetbl

4 He does his homework on his _____. ptlopa mopetcur

THINK BIG

Which electronic device is most useful for doing homework? Why?

_____

Which electronic device is best for playing games? Why?

_____

Reading | Science fiction

5 Listen and read. Then answer the questions.

Jenny's Bad Morning

Jenny, a Year 6 pupil, was sleeping when her bed started shaking. While the bed was shaking, a strange voice said, "Jenny, wake up! Time to go to school!" "You'll wake everybody up! Stop shaking and talking!" Jenny said. "Sorry," said the bed.

"I'm hungry," said Jenny. "Good morning, Jenny," a robot chair said. She sat on the robot and patted it. The robot carried her to the kitchen. "What would you like for breakfast, Jenny?" asked the fridge.

Jenny said, "Crunchy Crisp Cereal and toast, please." Five seconds later, the fridge opened up and put a bowl of cold cereal in front of her and the toaster added hot toast with butter.

After breakfast, Jenny sat on the robot chair again and it took her to her room. Jenny got dressed. "These clothes are too tight," said Jenny. The robot said, "Clothes, be bigger." The clothes got a little bigger. "Perfect!" said Jenny.

It was time for school. Jenny's mum said, "Hurry up, Jenny, get in the Fly Car." "Fly Car? No one rides in Fly Cars any more," thought Jenny. Jenny wanted to use a Flying Suit to fly her to school. Her mum shook her head. "Sorry, you can't use a Flying Suit until you're 12." Jenny got in the Fly Car. She wasn't happy. She hated being 11! She thought, "I want to be 12! It'll be so much more fun."

1 How does Jenny wake up?

_____

2 Who makes Jenny's breakfast?

_____

3 How does Jenny get to school?

_____

4 Does Jenny like the Fly Car? Why/Why not?

_____

6 Answer the questions.

Would you like Jenny's life? Why/Why not?

_____

_____

2:34

7 Listen. Then answer the questions.

Mum:	Jason, <u>come on</u>. It's time to get ready for school.
Jason:	Oh, Mum. Do I have to?
Mum:	Yes! Get your books ready while I <u>log on</u> to your virtual classroom.
Jason:	OK. <u>Whoops!</u> I'm nearly late for my English lesson!
Mum:	At least you don't have to take the bus for an hour to school any more. Your teacher's right here for you all the time. You just need to <u>switch</u> him <u>on</u>!
Jason:	Yes. But this robot teacher is stricter than the human ones were!
Mum:	That's good. Maybe you'll learn more!

1 Where is Jason?

_____

2 Where does Jason go to school?

_____

3 How does Jason start classes with his teacher?

_____

4 Why does Jason prefer human teachers to robot teachers?

_____

8 Look at 7. Read the underlined expressions. How can you say them in other words? Match and write the letter.

_____	**1** come on	**a**	I'm surprised.
_____	**2** log on	**b**	Hurry! Let's go.
_____	**3** Whoops!	**c**	start the computer
_____	**4** switch on	**d**	turn on

9 Complete the dialogue with the expressions in 8.

Mum:	¹_____, Emma. It's three o'clock. You'll be late for the football game.
Emma:	Mum! The game was at two! I've missed it!
Mum:	²_____! Sorry, Emma. Never mind, it's raining anyway.
Emma:	That's OK. I'll ³_____ to my laptop and play online.
Mum:	Good idea. I'll ⁴_____ the lights for you. It's getting dark.

Language in Action

Do you think we'**ll have** cars 100 years from now?

Yes, we **will**. But cars **won't have** drivers! They'**ll** use computers.

No, we **won't**. We'**ll have** spaceships.

10 Look at the pictures. Complete the sentences. Use will or won't. Then listen and check your answers.

1 In 2020, smartphones _____ look the same as they do today.

2 In the future, you _____ wear your phone on your wrist.

3 In a few years from now, you _____ carry your computer in your pocket.

4 In the future, people _____ carry large tablets any more.

5 In the future, people probably _____ listen to music on an mp3 player.

6 With one Patchster patch near each ear, you and your friends _____ be able to listen to the same music at the same time.

11 Complete the questions and answers. Use will and won't.

1 Do you think computers _____ roll up like a piece of paper in the future?

_____

2 Do you think smartphones _____ be as smart as you?

_____

3 Do you think tablets _____ be bigger than they are today?

_____

4 Do you think robots _____ tidy your room for you?

_____

Who **will use** video messaging in the future?	**Anyone** with a computer and internet access will use video messaging.
Who **will send** letters to communicate with friends in the future?	**No one/Nobody** will send letters to communicate with friends. **Everyone/Everybody** will use email. Well, **someone** might write a letter!

12 Read the class survey.

Mrs Brown's Class Survey — Which activities will we do in 2020?	
Will we . . .	Percentage of people who say "yes"
1. drive solar-powered cars?	100%
2. read paper books?	10%
3. go to Mars on a spaceship for a holiday?	0%
4. use non-digital cameras?	0%
5. send paper birthday cards?	20%

Mrs Brown's class survey predicts that the following statements will come true. Circle the correct words.

1 _____ will drive solar-powered cars.

  a Everybody   **b** Someone

2 _____ will read paper books.

  a No one   **b** Someone

3 _____ will go to Mars on a spaceship for a holiday.

  a Someone   **b** Nobody

4 _____ will use non-digital cameras. We'll take pictures with digital cameras and smartphones.

  a No one   **b** Someone

5 _____ who likes to write will send paper birthday cards. Everyone else will send email cards.

  a Nobody   **b** Anyone

13 Circle the sentences in 13 that you agree with. Write one sentence that you don't agree with. Explain why.

I don't think that _____ because _____.

14 Read. How will running robots help police?

TOMORROW'S ROBOTS

We all know that robots will be part of our future. In fact, in some factories, robots already make a lot of things. We aren't sure what these robotic creatures of the future will do but many will surely be socially assistive robots. They will help us do things that are too dangerous for people to do. That's good, isn't it?

Firefighter Robots
One day, there will be robots that fight fires. Human firefighters will control the robots and guide them into burning buildings. One type of robot will look like a real firefighter. These robots will be able to walk, climb up ladders and see through smoke. Another type will look like a snake, able to move through the air. These will help firefighters find people trapped in small spaces.

Running Robots
There might also be some robots that look like animals. They'll probably have four legs and be able to run very fast. They'll have bigger back legs than front legs so that they can jump, too. These robots will probably help police catch criminals. They'll catch the criminals because they'll be able to run faster than humans.

Jumping Robots
This robot won't look like an animal or a person but it'll do amazing things. It'll have wheels that move it from place to place. What's amazing about this robot is that it'll be able to jump very high. In fact it might be able to jump over walls or onto rooftops. It'll help police see if there are dangerous things or people there.

15 Read 14 again and complete the chart.

Robot	What It Will Be Able To Do	Who and How It Will Help
1 Firefighter Robot		
2 Running Robot		
3 Jumping Robot		

THINK BIG

Which of the robots in 14 do you think will help people the most? Why?

_____

_____

16 Read. How many people can speak the Khang language?

SAVING LANGUAGES: NOW AND LONG AGO

Khang: Vietnam

The Khang language and culture is one of the most endangered in Vietnam. There are only 4,000 speakers and they haven't got a written language. UNESCO (United Nations Educational, Scientific and Cultural Organization) decided to help keep the Khang language and culture from disappearing. UNESCO workers wrote down Khang traditions, developed an alphabet, prepared materials for teaching the language in classes and trained local speakers to teach those classes.

17 Read 16 again and circle T for true or F for false.

1	The Khang language always had an alphabet.	**T**	**F**
2	The Khang people are studying their language in classes today.	**T**	**F**
3	Teaching the Khang language to young people will make the language endangered.	**T**	**F**

18 Answer the questions.

1 What languages do you want to speak well? _____

_____

2 What ways can people help save endangered languages? _____

_____

_____

3 Would you like to learn Khang? Why/Why not? _____

_____

_____

4 Imagine you are the last speaker of a language. What do you want people to know about your language? _____

_____

_____

A diary is a special notebook. People often write about their day in this notebook. They write about the things that happened and they often write about their feelings or thoughts during the day. Many people like writing in their diary every day. Some people share their diary entries. Some people write only for themselves. A diary entry is similar to a letter. It includes:

- a greeting (*Dear Diary, Hello*)
- an opening sentence. It usually describes the topic of your entry. (*I'm very happy today.*)
- the body. It includes information about the topic.
- a closing (*Goodnight, Love, Bye*)
- your name

19 Label the parts of the diary entry.

1 _____ Dear Diary,

2 _____ We learnt about the future today in school.

3 _____ I started thinking about my life in the future. In five

years, everyone in my class will be in the sixth form. I

hope I'll have a boyfriend and that he's nice! I won't be

able to drive but I hope that Mum and Dad will let me

stay out late. I'm tired now so I'll say goodbye.

4 _____ Goodnight,

5 _____ Pat

20 Look at 19. Circle the correct answers.

1 What comes after the greeting?   **a** a full stop (.)   **b** a comma (,)   **c** nothing

2 What comes after the closing?   **a** a full stop (.)   **b** a comma (,)   **c** nothing

3 What comes after the writer's name? **a** a full stop (.)   **b** a comma (,)   **c** nothing

21 Imagine your life in six years' time. Write a diary entry about you and your life. Use 19 and 20 to help you.

THINK BIG Which is the odd one out?

diary / blog / shopping list / letter

22 Look at the chart. Then complete the sentences. Use will or won't.

My Predictions for the Year 2020	I don't think we'll have these things! Bye-bye!	I think these things will definitely be here!
1 text friends	with mobile phones	with smartphones
2 write essays	on laptops – parents might use them	on tablets
3 listen to music	on mp3 players	on Patchster-like devices
4 buy items	mostly online using computers	mostly online using electronic gadgets

1 I think people _____ with mobile phones. We _____ with smartphones.

2 We _____ on tablets in 2020. We _____ on laptops.

3 In the future, we _____ on mp3 players. We _____ with Patchster-like devices.

4 I think we _____ mostly online using our electronic gadgets.
We _____ online using computers.

23 Look at 22. Complete the sentences. Use Everybody or Nobody.

1 _____ will use mobile phones.

2 _____ will write essays on laptops.

3 _____ will use Patchster-like devices.

4 _____ will listen to music on mp3 players.

24 Answer the questions. Use your own ideas.

1 Do you think people will carry umbrellas in the future? Why/Why not?

_____

2 Do you think we'll read only ebooks in the year 2025 instead of paper books? Why/Why not?

_____

1 Look at the pictures. What are they? Write the words.

SHOPPING AROUND

1 _____
2 _____
3 _____
4 _____

HOLIDAY TIME

1 _____ 2 _____
3 _____ 4 _____

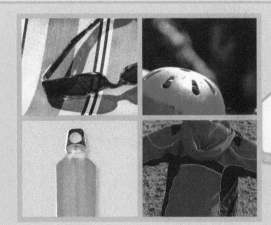

THE FUTURE

1 _____
2 _____
3 _____
4 _____

2 Find or think of a song that talks about shopping, a holiday or the future. Complete the chart.

Song title	
Singer	
Is the song in English? What language is the song in?	
What's it about?	
Why do you like listening to this song?	
Is it the most popular song now?	
What were you doing when you first heard it?	
Do you think it'll be popular next year?	

3 Write a review of the song for your school newspaper. Use the information in 1 and 2 to help you.

WHAT'S THAT?

1 Look at the pictures. Match the gadgets to their uses. Write the letters.

_____ **Picture 1** This is used for…

_____ **Picture 2** These are used for…

_____ **Picture 3** This is used for…

_____ **Picture 4** This is used for…

a listening to music. You wear this headband to listen to music comfortably, even while you sleep. It's a Music Headband.

b doing research. You ask it questions and it tells you the answers. It helps you find information. It's Robo-pedia.

c watching films. You put on these glasses and watch films that only you can see. They're Cinema Glasses.

d drinking. You can fill it up with water and drink it. When you are finished, you can roll it up and put it away. It's a Roll-up Bottle.

2 Which gadgets in 1 do you like? Rate them. 1 = It's amazing! 2 = It's cool. 3 = It's OK. 4 = It's boring/not interesting.

a Robo-pedia _____   **b** Roll-up Bottle _____

c Cinema Glasses _____   **d** Music Headband _____

3 Match the old things to the modern things. Write the numbers.

1 2 3 4

a b c d

____   ____   ____   ____

4 *3:04* Write the names. Use the words in the box. Listen and circle the correct answers.

| handheld game device | instant camera | mobile phone | transistor radio |

1 A _____ is used to

  a play video games at home.   **b** play games outside.

2 A _____ is used mostly to

  a talk to people.   **b** record messages.

3 An _____ is used mostly to

  a take photos.   **b** make films.

4 A _____ is used to

  a record music and the news.   **b** listen to music and the news.

What do you think about the future of these items? Will we still use them in the future? Why/Why not?

THINK BIG

| maps | telephone directories | watches |

_____

_____

5 Listen and read. Then answer the questions.

CAST

Ann, Jim (classmates) | Miss Albany (teacher)

SETTING: A Year 6 classroom in the year 2015.
[The class finds a time capsule that the school made in 1990.
They open it and are looking at the things inside it.]

Ann:	*[picking up a thin square object]* Look at this. What is it?
Jim:	*[takes it from her and looks at it carefully]* I'm not sure. It's plastic and it's got a metal rectangle on it.
Ann:	Hmm… I think it was used for watching films on a computer.
Jim:	I don't think so. I don't think people could watch films on computers in 1990.
Ann:	You're right.
Jim:	*[picking up a thick rectangular object]* And what's this? It's some kind of small machine.
Ann:	*[presses one of the buttons and it starts working]* Hey, it's an old music player. *[Ann puts the headphones to her ears]*
Jim:	*[putting his hands over his ears]* Oh, no! I don't want to listen to old music!
Ann:	*[laughing]* Someone's going to say the same thing about our music in the future. I kind of like this music. I'm going to take it to my grandad. He might remember this kind of music.

[A teacher enters]

Jim:	*[holding up the thin square object]* Hello, Miss Albany. What's this?
Miss Albany:	Oh, that's a floppy disk. People used them to keep information on from a computer. That way they had the information even if their computer got lost.
Jim:	I see.
Ann:	It's fun looking at these old things.

1 What did Ann pick up?

_____

2 What did she think it was used for?

_____

3 Did Jim like the music?

_____

4 What did people use the square object for?

_____

6 Answer the questions.

How old does something have to be for you to think it is 'old'? Why?

_____

3:09

7 Listen and read. Circle T for true or F for false.

Iris: What's in the box?

Laura: It's not a box. <u>See?</u> It doesn't open. My grandad brought it back from China when he went there many years ago.

Iris: <u>Let's see.</u> It's hard and looks like it would break if you dropped it.

Laura: Well, it would! It's ceramic, like the plates and dishes we use for eating.

Iris: OK. But what is it? What's it used for?

Laura: <u>You won't believe it</u> but it's a pillow!

Iris: A pillow? But it's so hard!

Laura: A long time ago, women in Asia had very beautiful hairstyles that took a lot of work to create. They didn't want to ruin them by sleeping on a soft pillow. So they just rested their necks on a ceramic pillow like this one. It was used for <u>keeping their hair in place</u>.

Iris: Gosh! That doesn't sound very comfortable.

1	The object is a pillow made of plastic.	T	F
2	It was used when women were sleeping.	T	F
3	Iris thinks it's a good pillow.	T	F

8 Look at 7. Read the underlined expressions. How can you say them in other words? Match and write the letters.

_____ **1** See?

_____ **2** You won't believe it.

_____ **3** Let's see.

_____ **4** keep (their hair) in place

a It's surprising.

b Look closely.

c keep (their hair) from getting messy

d Let me think.

9 Complete the dialogue. Use the expressions in 8.

A: What were those bones used for?

B: ¹_____. Now I remember. ²_____ but those bones were used for a children's game called *knucklebones*!

A: How did women in ancient Greece ³_____ their clothes _____?

B: Well, look at this picture. ⁴_____? They wrapped a piece of cloth around themselves and used pins or belts.

Language in Action

What's it **used for**?	It's **used for** listening to music. It's **used to** listen to music.

10 Match and write the letters.

_____ **1** A hands-free ear piece is used for

_____ **2** A mobile phone is used to

_____ **3** A video game system is used to

_____ **4** A handheld game device is used for

a play video games.

b making phone calls.

c playing video games.

d make phone calls.

11 Look and read. Answer the questions with used for or used to and the words from the box.

finding where a place is   listen to music   make cars go   writing essays

1

A: What are they used for?

B: _____

2

A: What are they used for?

B: _____

3

A: What's it used for?

B: _____

4

A: What's it used for?

B: _____

| What is it? | I'm not sure. It **may** be a small plate. |
| | It **might** be a salt dish. |

12 What do you think these old things are? Use the words from the box and may or might to write sentences.

abacus   egg beater   gramophone   washboard

1 _____

2 _____

3 _____

4 _____

13 Look at the items in 12. What do you think they were used for? Write sentences with used to.

1 _____

2 _____

3 _____

4 _____

14 Complete the chart with inventions. Use the words from the box.

> candle   cash register   combustion engine   plumbing

How the inventions help people	Invention
1 We can easily have a shower and wash dishes and clothes.	
2 We can travel by vehicles on land, sea and air.	
3 We can see at night when the lights go out.	
4 Shops can keep their money safely.	

15 Read. Who invented the bendable straw?

Everyday Inventions

Who do you think of when you hear the word *inventor*? Do you think of Thomas Edison, the inventor of the light bulb, or Karl Benz, the inventor of the petrol-powered car?

Not all inventors are world-famous. In fact, we don't know the names of a lot of inventors who invented some of the small, useful things we use every day. For example, everyone knows about the bendable straw. But does anyone know the name Joseph Friedman? In 1937, he invented the bendable straw.

bendable straw

Joseph's brother owned a café. One day, Joseph was watching his youngest daughter drink a milkshake with a long straw. The straw was long and she couldn't reach the end of it easily with her mouth. You may not see this as a problem but Joseph did! He said, "Let's see. I'll put a metal screw into the straw, and wrap some wire around it on the outside of the straw." He tried it and then he took the screw out. The straw could bend and the bendable straw was born.

16 Read **15** again and answer the questions.

1 Who was with Joseph Friedman at his brother's café? _____

2 What problem was she having? _____

3 What did Joseph Friedman put inside and outside the straw? _____

4 What was the result? _____

17 Read. What part of a bullet train is like a kingfisher's beak?

Animals Inspire Inventions

Animals move in ways that are unique. People can't swim like dolphins or turn their heads around like owls. Scientists are using computer technology to study the movement of animals. Then they use this knowledge to create interesting inventions that help people.

Elephant-Inspired Arm and Hand

Engineers in England studied the elephant's trunk. They wanted to create a robotic arm and hand that could move just like an arm and could work safely with humans in factories and other places. They created a bionic handling assistant. The assistant looks like an elephant's trunk with a claw and is very light and very safe. When it accidentally hits a human, it moves back. It's also very gentle. It can pick up an egg!

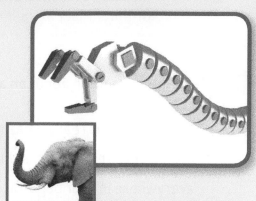

Kingfisher-Inspired Train

A Japanese engineer, Eiji Nakatsu, wanted to solve a problem. The fastest trains in Japan, the bullet trains, made a very loud noise when they came out of tunnels. Trains also slowed down when they came out of tunnels. Eiji loved birds and he knew that kingfishers dive into the water from the air with no splash. This is because of the shape of their beaks. He worked to change the front of the trains to be more like a kingfisher beak. The problem was solved.

These are just two inventions inspired by animals. So the next time you see an animal, look at it closely. There might be an invention inspired by it!

18 Read 17 again and circle T for true or F for false.

1 An elephant leg inspired the bionic handling assistant.　　T　　F

2 The bionic handling assistant is used in factories.　　T　　F

3 The kingfisher-inspired trains make a noise when they come
out of tunnels.　　T　　F

4 The back of the train is the shape of a kingfisher beak.　　T　　F

THINK BIG

Which invention in 17 do you think is the most interesting? Why?

_____

_____

When you write a description of an object, it's good to write about:

- the way it looks (**It's** red, large and round. **It looks like** an elephant's trunk.)
- the things it's got and can do (**It's got** two legs. **It can** go very fast.)
- what it's used for (**It's used to** carry heavy things.)

Include as much information as you can so the readers can see a picture of that object in their mind.

19 Read this paragraph about an amazing object. What is it?

This object is really amazing. It's rectangular. It's white or black with a large screen on one side. It looks like a thin book but you can't open or close it. You can carry it everywhere in your bag. You can read and listen to music on it. It's got a camera so you can take pictures and even videos with it. You can also send and receive emails on it. It's used to entertain people on long trips. It's a _____.

20 Underline the sentences in 19 that describe the way the object looks. Circle the sentences that describe the things it has got/can do. Underline twice the things it is used for.

21 Think of an invention. Complete the idea web.

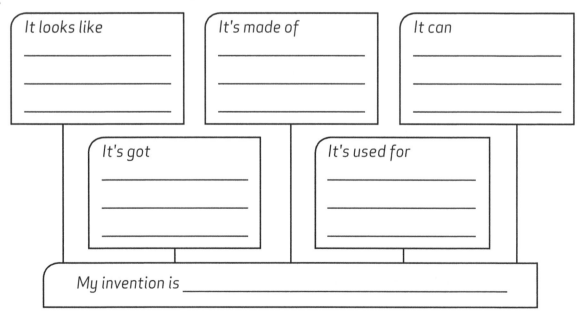

It looks like
_____
_____
_____

It's made of
_____
_____
_____

It can
_____
_____
_____

It's got
_____
_____
_____

It's used for
_____
_____
_____

My invention is _____

22 Write a description of an invention in your notebook. Use 19, 20 and 21 to help you.

23 Look at the code. Write the words. Then match the words and pictures. Write the numbers.

●	▲	■	▬	✦	◈	⬈	⬇	➤	◄	=	+	÷
a	b	c	d	e	f	g	h	i	j	k	l	m

x	○	◇	□	▭	*	!	]	?	#	%	▼	◢
n	o	p	q	r	s	t	u	v	w	x	y	z

1 ⬇ ● x ▬ * - ◈ ▭ ✦ ✦   ✦ ● ▭   ◇ ➤ ✦ ■ ✦

‾ ‾ ‾ ‾ ‾   ‾ ‾ ‾ ‾   ‾ ‾ ‾ ‾ ‾

2 ➤ x * ! ● x !   ■ ● ÷ ✦ ▭ ●   a __

‾ ‾ ‾ ‾ ‾ ‾ ‾   ‾ ‾ ‾ ‾ ‾ ‾

3 ! ▭ ● x * ➤ * ! ○ ▭   ▭ ● ▬ ➤   b __

‾ ‾ ‾ ‾ ‾ ‾ ‾ ‾ ‾ ‾   ‾ ‾ ‾ ‾

c __

24 Imagine it's the year 2023. How will you talk about these things? Write the questions. Complete the answers. Use used to and used for and the words from the box.

> finding where a place is   listen to music   making cars go   play fun games

1 **A:** These are _____.

   B: _____?

   A: They'_____.

2 **A:** This is a _____.

   B: _____?

   A: They're _____.

3 **A:** This is a _____.

   B: _____?

   A: It's _____.

4 **A:** This is a _____.

   B: _____?

   A: It's _____.

unit 8 WHERE DO THEY COME FROM?

1 Look at the pictures. Read the name of the inventions that come from these places. Do any surprise you?

Italy: eyeglasses, radio, piano

India: chess, ink, pyjamas

England: jigsaw puzzle, matches, combustion engine

China: sunglasses, noodles, paper lantern

2 Circle the inventions that you use or see every day.

jigsaw puzzle	chess	matches	eyeglasses
combustion engine	ink	pyjamas	piano
noodles	radio	chess	paper lantern

3 Look at 1 and 2. Where do most of the items that you circled come from?

Most of the products that I use or see were invented in _____.

4 What items that you use every day were invented in your country?

_____

5 Read. Circle the two correct answers.

1 These are made mostly of metal.

  a silver earrings   **b** a plane   **c** a basketball

2 These are made of rubber.

  a kitchen gloves   **b** T-shirts   **c** rain boots

3 Some of these are made of wool.

  a candles   **b** blankets   **c** jumpers

4 Some of these are made of cotton.

  a T-shirts   **b** jackets   **c** tyres

5 These are made of clay.

  a cups   **b** blankets   **c** plates

 3:19 **6** Listen. What are the things? Number them in the order you hear them. Then write the names.

| balls | clothes | teacup | train |

☐ _____   ☐ _____

☐ _____   ☐ _____

THINK BIG Clothes are made of a lot of different materials. Which materials can keep us warm? Which material can keep us dry?

_____

Reading | Travel forum

7 Listen and read. Then answer the questions.

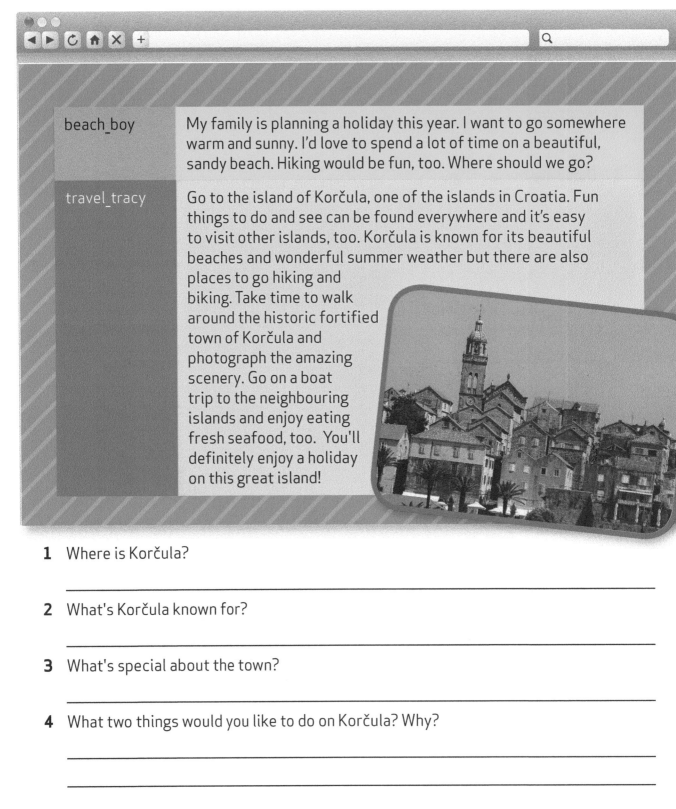

beach_boy My family is planning a holiday this year. I want to go somewhere warm and sunny. I'd love to spend a lot of time on a beautiful, sandy beach. Hiking would be fun, too. Where should we go?

travel_tracy Go to the island of Korčula, one of the islands in Croatia. Fun things to do and see can be found everywhere and it's easy to visit other islands, too. Korčula is known for its beautiful beaches and wonderful summer weather but there are also places to go hiking and biking. Take time to walk around the historic fortified town of Korčula and photograph the amazing scenery. Go on a boat trip to the neighbouring islands and enjoy eating fresh seafood, too. You'll definitely enjoy a holiday on this great island!

1 Where is Korčula?

_____

2 What's Korčula known for?

_____

3 What's special about the town?

_____

4 What two things would you like to do on Korčula? Why?

_____

_____

_____

8 Listen and read. Then circle T for true or F for false.

Suzy: Maybe I can find something for my sister here. It's her birthday next week.

Rosa: I definitely think you can. That table over there has <u>stacks of</u> <u>handmade</u> cotton blouses. They're made in Hungary.

Suzy: They're beautiful.

Rosa: Look, Margaret's wearing one. See how it's worn? The strings are pulled and tied in the front. It's a nice look.

Suzy: My sister would love it! But look, the one that I like is torn.

Rosa: I'm sure it can be mended. Look, the sign says, "These are all <u>second-hand</u> clothes." Let's ask Margaret's mum if it can be repaired.

Suzy: Brilliant idea!

1	It's Suzy's mum's birthday soon.	T	F
2	Rosa likes the blouses.	T	F
3	Suzy thinks her sister will like the blouse.	T	F
4	The blouse Suzy likes is new.	T	F

9 Look at 8. Read the underlined expressions. Match the expressions to their meaning. Write the letters.

_____ **1** stacks of

_____ **2** handmade

_____ **3** second-hand

a not new – having been worn in the past by someone else

b a lot of

c made by using your hands and not by machines in a factory

10 Complete the dialogue with the expressions in 9.

A: Look at these amazing scarves. Why are they so cheap?

B: I imagine it's because they're ¹_____. But they look new.

A: I'm going to buy the red and yellow one.

B: I love this local craft fair. ²_____ these things look ³_____!

A: I know. I love things that are made by hand.

| That watch **is made** in Switzerland. | The first pizza **was** probably **made** in Italy. |
| Those bananas **are grown** in Ecuador. | The first noodles **were** probably **made** in China. |

11 Match the three forms of the verbs. Draw lines.

Present Simple	Past Simple	Past Participle
1 eat	flew	flown
2 fly	made	invented
3 grow	ate	raised
4 introduce	invented	grown
5 invent	mined	eaten
6 produce	introduced	made
7 make	produced	introduced
8 mine	raised	mined
9 raise	grew	produced

12 Complete the sentences. Use the present simple passive form of the verb in brackets.

1 Olives _____. (grow in Greece)

2 Sheep _____. (raise in New Zealand)

3 Many cars _____. (make in China)

4 Gold _____. (mine in South Africa)

5 Denim _____. (produce in many countries)

13 Look. Complete the sentences. Use the past simple passive form of the verb in brackets.

1 Chess _____ probably _____ in India. (invent)

2 In 1783, the first hot air balloon _____. (fly)

3 The first shopping trolley _____ in 1937. (make)

4 The gramophone, or record player, _____ in 1877 by Thomas Edison. (introduce)

14 Unscramble the words. Use the words to write sentences. Use the present simple passive form of the verb.

1 anabsan   wrog

_____ _____

_____ in Ecuador.

2 lhsels   ndfi

_____ _____

_____ on the beach.

3 tfoolbal   lypa

_____ _____

_____ all over the world.

4 tobos   emka

_____ _____

_____ of rubber.

15 Read. What makes a farmers' market fun?

Farmers' Markets and Our Future

Farmers all over the world gather on specific days in specific places, like a park or car park, to sell their produce directly to customers. Some farmers' markets have live entertainment like singers or musicians and sell things other than produce, like crafts made by local people. So they can be really fun places!

Shopping at a farmers' market is a good thing to do. Here's why:

1. You can meet local farmers and learn about their produce.

2. Locally grown food is very fresh. So every bite tastes good!

3. The food doesn't have to travel a long distance from the farm to a distribution centre and then to you. It goes only a short distance from the farm to you. This results in less pollution and helps keep the environment clean.

4. Buying from local farmers can help the environment in other ways, too. When farmers don't make enough money to live, they are often obliged to sell their farms to land developers. The developers build houses and buildings on the farmland. More houses may cause more pollution.

5. A typical farm is a beautiful place. It has fields, meadows, woods and ponds. It provides a home for animals like rabbits, birds and deer. So if the farm disappears, the animals may have nowhere to live.

Next time your mum buys vegetables, think about asking her to go to a local farmers' market. You'll have a fun time.

16 Read 15 again and circle the correct answers.

1 Farmers' markets are always _____.

   a in different places   **b** in the same place

2 Buying locally helps the environment because _____.

   a farmers sell the produce cheaply   **b** produce travels a short distance from the farm to the market

3 If farmers can't get enough money to live, they might _____.

   a sell their farms   **b** build houses

4 If farmers sell their farms, _____.

   a animals will be able to stay on the land   **b** some animals will lose their home

17 Read. Why do people invent things?

Problems and Inventions

Why do people invent things? Where do ideas for inventions come from? There's a saying that 'Necessity is the mother of invention.' This means that people invent things because there's a problem and they want to solve the problem.

In 1912, Otto Frederick Rohwedder had an idea. He wanted to invent a machine that could slice a whole loaf of bread. He built his first bread slicer in 1917 but it was destroyed in a fire. In 1927, he had enough money to build another one. But he realised that he had a problem – the bread became stale after it was cut. He then had another idea and he built a bread slicer that sliced the bread and then wrapped it so that it wouldn't get stale so quickly.

Hacky Sack or Footbag is a fun sport that was invented by John Stalberger and Mike Marshall. In 1972, Mike Marshall made a small beanbag and kicked it in the air with his foot for fun. That same year John Stalberger had knee surgery. His knee exercises after surgery were boring so he looked for a more fun way to exercise. He and Mike shared ideas and the game of Hacky Sack was born.

Society needs inventors. Our lives are better because inventors are problem solvers. Think of a problem. Can you invent something to solve it?

18 Read 17 again and answer the questions.

1 What did Otto Frederick Rohwedder invent?

_____

2 What problem did he have?

_____

3 How did he solve the problem?

_____

4 What problem did John Stalberger have?

_____

5 How did he and Mike Marshall solve this problem?

_____

THINK BIG

What's the biggest problem in your home? What could you invent to solve it?

_____

When you write a persuasive paragraph, you want your reader to agree with your opinion. A good persuasive paragraph gives a strong main opinion and reasons for that opinion. Your reasons make your opinion stronger and more believable.

Opinion: *The South of France is a perfect place for a holiday.*

Reasons: *It's got beautiful beaches with wonderful swimming and lovely scenery.*

There are lovely street markets and the local food is delicious.

There are interesting and historic towns to visit, too, such as Nice and Montpellier.

19 **Read the persuasive paragraph. Then answer the questions.**

[1]Cape Town is famous all over the world because it's a wonderful holiday destination. It's located at the tip of Africa in South Africa. [2]You won't be bored here because there are lots of fun things to do. [3]You can swim and sunbathe at Camps Bay, a favourite beach, and you can surf here, too. [4]You can go on bus tours around the city or boat tours to see dolphins, seals and humpback whales. [5]You can also hike up Table Mountain or go up in a cable car. The view from the top is amazing! [6]Cape Town is full of wonderful adventures for everyone. Why not choose it for your next holiday?

1 Which sentence is the main opinion? _____

2 How many reasons are given for that opinion? _____

3 Which sentences are the reasons? _____

4 Do you want to go there? Why/Why not? _____

20 **Think of a lovely holiday spot.**
Complete the chart with your ideas.

Explain your reason
_____
_____

Name the holiday spot
_____
_____
_____

Give your opinion
_____
_____

Give a second reason
_____
_____

Give a third reason
_____
_____

21 Use your chart in 20 to write a persuasive paragraph about your holiday spot.

Think of two reasons why people should visit your country for a holiday.

THINK
BIG
_____
_____

22 Circle the products that can be made of the materials in the chart.

Wool	Rubber	Cotton	Metal	Clay
rug	comb	plate	shopping trolley	pottery
scarf	boots	towels	cola can	produce
cola can	paper	jeans	watch	bowls
blanket	tyre	plane	food	flower pot

23 Read and circle the correct answers.

1 Coffee _____ in Costa Rica and you can visit coffee farms there.

   a was grown   **b** is grown

2 Beautiful glass _____ in Italy. You can buy it in expensive shops.

   a was made   **b** is made

3 Chocolate nut bars _____ in Canada.

   a were created   **b** are created

4 Fantastic watches _____ in Switzerland and shops all over the world sell them.

   a are made   **b** were made

5 A lot of cattle _____ in Argentina today.

   a were raised   **b** are raised

6 The jigsaw puzzle _____ by an Englishman in 1767.

   a was invented   **b** is invented

24 Complete the sentences with the correct form of the verb in brackets.

1 Jars _____ from glass. (make)

2 Apples _____ in Italy and are very popular in the autumn. (grow)

3 Matches _____ in England in 1827. (invent)

4 The earliest noodles _____ in China a long, long time ago. (eat)

HOW ADVENTUROUS ARE YOU?

1 Listen and match. Write the number.

a

b

c

d

2 Read about the food in the pictures in 1. Rate them 1 = I really want to try it! 2 = I might want to try it. 3 = I never want to try it! Write your ratings.

1 This Filipino dessert is called Buko Pandan. It looks pretty and it's got a wonderful, sweet taste.

2 Tandoori chicken is a popular traditional dish from India. It is made with chicken and spices like pepper and curry. It tastes hot and spicy!

3 Chinese soup has got tofu in it. It's hot and sour. It's got a very unusual taste!

4 Marinated octopus is a traditional seafood from Greece. The octopus is left in olive oil, lemon juice and herbs for a short time. It's delicious!

3 How adventurous with food are you? Look at your ratings and ✓ your answer.

☐ I'm very adventurous. I rated most of the food a **1**.

☐ I'm quite adventurous. I rated most of the food a **2**.

☐ I'm not adventurous at all. I rated most of the food a **3**.

4 Listen and ✓ the words you hear for each food.

	unusual	tasty	popular	raw	spicy	sweet	traditional	delicious
1 gazpacho								
2 sushi								
3 tagine								
4 spumoni								

5 What food do you like? What food don't you like? What does it taste like?

_____

_____

THINK
BIG

Name a traditional food from your country. Then circle words to describe it.

_____

hot / raw / sweet / spicy / cold / sour

unusual / popular / delicious

6 Listen and read. Then answer the questions.

LIFE ON a BOAT

Eleven-year-old Glenn Dodd has lived on a boat with his family for the past two years. A local radio station is interviewing him.

Interviewer: Today on *Awesome Adventures*, we're talking to 11-year-old Glenn Dodd. Glenn's family has lived on a boat and has travelled around Australia for the last two years. Tell me, Glenn, what's it like living on a boat?

Glenn Dodd: Well, in the beginning it was really hard. There are four people in my family and a dog. The boat is small so we were always very close to each other.

Interviewer: Wow! I'm sure that was tough sometimes.

Glenn Dodd: Yes, we had to learn to get along or my dad said he'd throw us into the sea!

Interviewer: That would make me behave, too! What do you like the most about life on a boat?

Glenn Dodd: Well, probably all the new things I can try.

Interviewer: Like what? Give me an example.

Glenn Dodd: Well, I've eaten alligator meat a few times. And I've scuba dived with stingrays. That was a bit scary!

Interviewer I can imagine it was! Now tell me, after two years, would you rather live on a boat or in a house?

Glenn Dodd: Honestly, I really want to live in a house now, like my friends. Actually, my family has decided to go back home next month. So, soon, I'm going to be a land creature again.

Interviewer: Well, good luck, Glenn. That's all the time we have. Thanks again for sharing your story.

1 Where does Glenn Dodd live now? _____

2 What does Glenn like most about living there? _____

3 Do you think Glenn is an adventurous person? Why/Why not? _____

4:09

7 Listen. Then circle the correct answers.

Allie: Hi, Roberto. Let's <u>do something</u> on Saturday afternoon.

Roberto: <u>That sounds good</u>, Allie. But I have a lesson on Saturday.

Allie: You have lessons on Saturdays?

Roberto: Yes. I'm learning Chinese!

Allie: Chinese? Really?

Roberto: Yes. It's really interesting. Have you ever studied another language?

Allie: Well, I can speak English and Spanish. But I've never studied another language.

Roberto: It's a lot of fun. And I'm learning a lot. I can say so many things in Chinese already.

Allie: <u>That's amazing!</u> How do you say *hello* in Chinese?

Roberto: Ni hao, Allie!

Allie: Hola, Roberto!

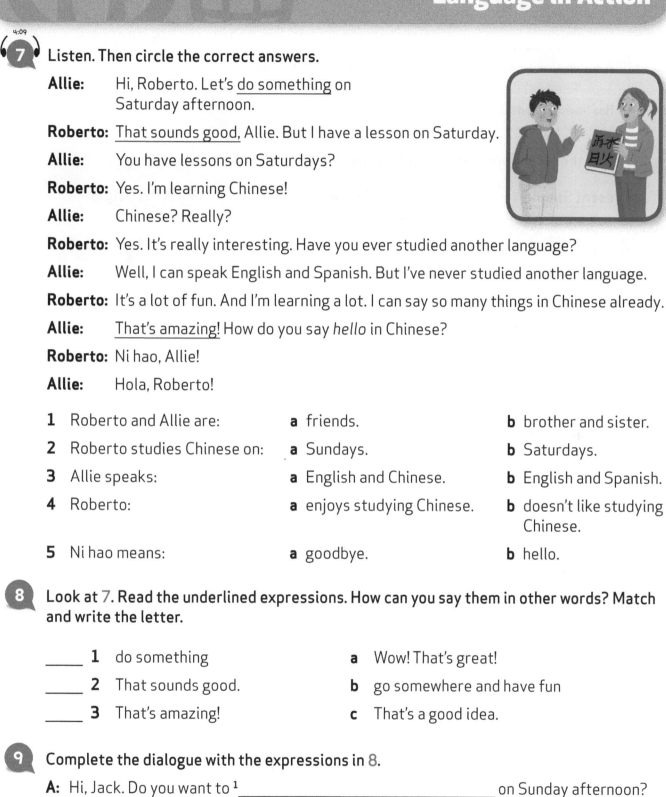

1 Roberto and Allie are:	**a** friends.	**b** brother and sister.
2 Roberto studies Chinese on:	**a** Sundays.	**b** Saturdays.
3 Allie speaks:	**a** English and Chinese.	**b** English and Spanish.
4 Roberto:	**a** enjoys studying Chinese.	**b** doesn't like studying Chinese.
5 Ni hao means:	**a** goodbye.	**b** hello.

8 Look at 7. Read the underlined expressions. How can you say them in other words? Match and write the letter.

_____ **1** do something   **a** Wow! That's great!

_____ **2** That sounds good.   **b** go somewhere and have fun

_____ **3** That's amazing!   **c** That's a good idea.

9 Complete the dialogue with the expressions in 8.

A: Hi, Jack. Do you want to ¹_____ on Sunday afternoon?

B: ²_____. Do you want to go to the cinema? I've got two tickets and they were free!

A: ³_____. Where did you get them from?

B: They were a present.

Language in Action

Have you ever been to a concert?	Yes, I have./No, I haven't.
Has he ever been skydiving?	Yes, he has./No, he hasn't.

10 Match the three forms of the verbs. Draw lines.

Present Simple	**Past Simple**	**Past Participle**
1 act	fell	gone
2 break	moved	fallen
3 fall	swam	won
4 go	broke	acted
5 have	acted	swum
6 move	won	broken
7 swim	went	had
8 win	had	moved

11 Unscramble the questions. Then look and write the answers.

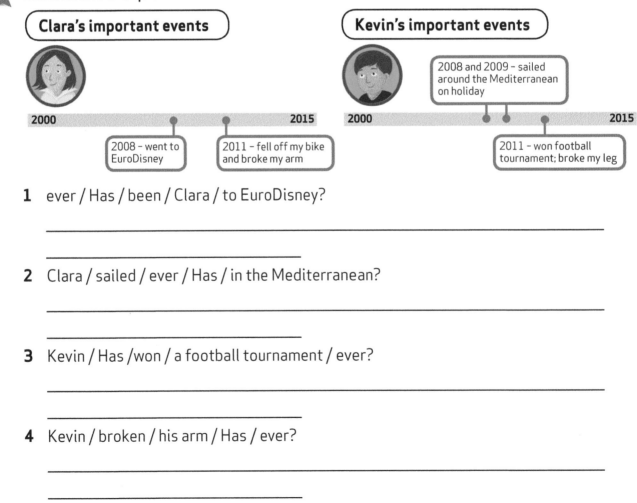

Clara's important events

2000   2015

2008 – went to EuroDisney

2011 – fell off my bike and broke my arm

Kevin's important events

2008 and 2009 – sailed around the Mediterranean on holiday

2000   2015

2011 – won football tournament; broke my leg

1 ever / Has / been / Clara / to EuroDisney?

_____

_____

2 Clara / sailed / ever / Has / in the Mediterranean?

_____

_____

3 Kevin / Has /won / a football tournament / ever?

_____

_____

4 Kevin / broken / his arm / Has / ever?

_____

_____

Would they **rather** play football or watch it?	They'**d rather** play football.

I'd = I would
you'd = you would
he'd = he would
she'd = she would
they'd = they would

12 Follow the lines. Make guesses and answer the questions.

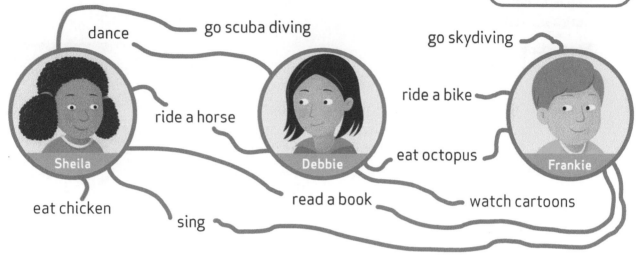

dance   go scuba diving   go skydiving

ride a bike

ride a horse

eat octopus

Sheila   Debbie   Frankie

eat chicken   read a book   watch cartoons

sing

1 Would Sheila rather go skydiving or go scuba diving?

_____

2 Would Sheila and Debbie rather ride a bike or ride a horse?

_____

3 Would Frank rather eat chicken or eat octopus?

_____

4 Would Frank and Sheila rather watch cartoons or read a book?

_____

13 Answer the questions for you.

1 Would you rather eat chicken or eat octopus?

_____

2 Would you rather ride a bike or ride a horse?

_____

3 Would you rather go skydiving or go scuba diving?

_____

14 Read. Why do some people race motorcycles at very high speeds?

Extreme Sports

Some people love the feel of adrenalin rushing through their bodies, giving them that extra boost of energy. This is called an adrenalin rush. People do many things to feel an adrenalin rush.

Freeriding

Freeriding is like big-wave surfing on snow. Skiers go to the very top of a high, steep mountain and ski down it. There are no paths for them to follow – they just follow the slopes and natural paths down the mountain. Where does the adrenalin rush come from? They go down the mountain very, very fast because the slopes that they ski down are very steep. Some slopes are almost at 90 degrees to the ground. They also fly high in the air in some places where they ski over snow-covered rock cliffs.

Motorcycle racing

All over the world, there are people who enjoy motorcycle riding. Some people travel across continents on motorcycles because they find it fun and it relieves stress. But others are not interested in relaxing – they want an adrenalin rush, so they race motorcycles at very high speeds. They ride around a track and on the straight part of the track they can go up to 300 kilometres per hour. When they go around a corner, they lean over so that their knees nearly touch the ground and they sometimes do that at about 200 kilometres per hour. That's fast!

15 Read 14 again and circle T for true or F for false.

1 Freeriders ski down very high, steep mountains.   T   F

2 Motorcycle racers can go faster around corners than on the   T   F
  straight part of the track.

3 Freeriders and motorcycle racers want an adrenalin rush.   T   F

4 Freeriders and motorcycle racers aren't adventurous.   T   F

5 Freeriders follow a path.   T   F

16 Read. How long did it take Laura to sail around the world?

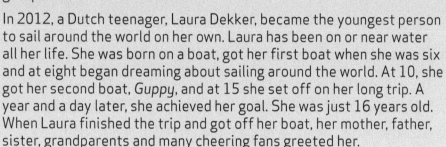

Jordan Romero is an amazing teenager who has climbed seven of the highest and most challenging mountains on seven continents. He climbed his first mountain, Mount Kilimanjaro in Africa, in 2006 when he was 10. He's the youngest person in the world to do this. In 2011, when he was 15, he climbed the last of the seven mountains, a mountain in Antarctica. Jordan, who lives in California, wants to help other children reach their goals so he started a group called *Find Your Everest*.

In 2012, a Dutch teenager, Laura Dekker, became the youngest person to sail around the world on her own. Laura has been on or near water all her life. She was born on a boat, got her first boat when she was six and at eight began dreaming about sailing around the world. At 10, she got her second boat, *Guppy*, and at 15 she set off on her long trip. A year and a day later, she achieved her goal. She was just 16 years old. When Laura finished the trip and got off her boat, her mother, father, sister, grandparents and many cheering fans greeted her.

17 Read 16 again and answer the questions.

1 How many mountains on how many continents has Jordan Romero climbed?

_____

2 How old was he when he climbed his last mountain?

_____

3 What does *Find Your Everest* do?

_____

4 How old was Laura when she got her first boat?

_____

5 How old was she when she set off to achieve her goal?

_____

6 At 16, what record did Laura set?

_____

Pretend that you could interview one of these teenagers. Which one would you interview? What two questions would you ask?

_____

_____

A good description includes:

- a clear topic sentence that tells the reader what you are going to write about. Example: *I'm not a risk taker.*
- more information about the topic that gives examples or details. You can introduce your examples using *For example.* Always use a comma. *For example, I don't like trying new foods. I also get nervous when I go to new places where I can't speak the language.*
- a summary that retells your topic sentence in a new way. Example: *It's OK that I'm not a risk taker because it's good to have different people in the world.*

18 Read the description. Then answer the questions. Write the numbers.

¹I'm not at all adventurous and I don't like to try new things. ²For example, I don't play sports because every time I've played, I've got hurt. ³I also don't like trying new foods and I prefer to eat the same food every day. ⁴This is strange because my whole family loves trying food from different cultures. ⁵Everyone says I should be more adventurous and try new things but I'm happy just the way I am.

_____ **1** Which sentence is the topic sentence?

_____ **2** Which sentences give details about the topic?

_____ **3** Which sentence retells the topic in a new way?

19 Think of ways that you are *not* adventurous. Complete the chart.

Complete the sentence: I am not adventurous because…
Give an example and details.
Give another example and details.
Write a summary. Explain in one sentence how you are not adventurous.

20 Write a paragraph about how you are *not* adventurous. Use 19 to help you.

21 **Find and circle these words.**

```
        q  z  i  w
     a  x  c  b  w  j  t  k
  n  o  m  v  d  q  y  r  f  d
  u  d  p  z  p  a  r  a  w  s
a  n  s  o  u  r  g  h  d  i  a  m
i  u  m  p  m  r  s  p  i  c  y  n
l  s  f  u  b  l  w  g  t  p  z  b
q  u  p  l  x  y  e  f  i  j  n  v
a  a  e  a  g  l  e  d  o  t  e  c
  l  q  r  w  q  t  s  n  y  u  s
     t  a  s  t  y  a  a  s  y
        i  m  v  l  j  l
```

popular
raw
sour
spicy
sweet
tasty
traditional
unusual

22 **Complete the sentences. Use some of the words in 21.**

1 One soup at the Spanish restaurant has a lot of spices in it. Not many people order it.

The soup is too _____ so it isn't _____.

2 Many of the dishes at the Greek restaurant are delicious seafood dishes. One of the dishes was eaten long ago, too.

That seafood dish is _____ and _____.

3 The new Mexican restaurant has a dessert that is made with avocado and lime.

The avocado pudding isn't common. It's _____. It isn't sweet like usual desserts. It's _____.

23 **Complete the sentences. Use the correct form of the verb in brackets. Then answer the questions for you.**

1 _____ you ever _____ to a Japanese restaurant? (be)

_____

2 _____ you ever _____ an octopus? (see)

_____

3 _____ you ever _____ curry? (eat)

_____

1 Unscramble and write the words. Add your own words on the extra lines.

GADGETS

1 _____
2 _____
3 _____
4 _____
5 _____

1 nattisn aecamr

2 hldenadh agem edievc

3 tniasrsort rdaoi

4 ivdoe aemg syetsm

PRODUCTS AND MATERIALS

1 _____
2 _____
3 _____
4 _____

1 tootnc janes

2 urrbeb botos

3 yacl

1 edusoiilc

2 lpruapo

3 tadiilnroat

4 uusulan

FOOD

1 _____
2 _____
3 _____
4 _____
5 _____

2 Find a song that talks about gadgets, products and materials or food. Complete the chart about the song.

Song title	
Who's the singer?	
Where does the singer come from?	
Who was the song written by?	
What's your favourite line in the song? Why is it your favourite?	
Would the singer rather sing traditional songs or popular songs?	
Has the song ever been a number one hit?	
Who else do you think might sing the song well?	

3 Write a note to your parents. Persuade them to let you go to a concert to hear this song and singer. Use the information in 1 and 2 to help you.

Unit 1 | Extra Grammar Practice

1 Read about Lisa and Dan. Complete the sentences with the correct words. Use the correct form of the verbs.

Lisa

"I'm in the drama club. I play the trumpet in the school orchestra. I can draw but I can't paint. Football is fun but basketball is boring."

"I'm in the Maths club. I want to learn how to do karate. Football is fun but basketball isn't fun. I can't draw."

Dan

1 Lisa is good at _____. (draw/paint)

2 Dan is interested in _____. (act/learn karate)

3 They aren't interested in _____. (draw/play basketball)

4 They enjoy _____. (play football/play basketball)

2 Look at 1. Complete the sentences with the words in brackets.

1 Lisa _____. (good at/paint)

2 Dan _____. (enjoy/draw)

3 Dan _____. (like/do Maths)

4 Lisa _____. (love/play the trumpet)

3 Look at 1. Complete the sentences with the correct form of the verbs in brackets.

1 **Lisa:** How about joining the art club?

   Dan: No, thanks. I _____. (like)

2 **Dan:** Do you want to join the Maths club?

   Lisa: I don't think so. I _____.
   (interested in)

3 **Emily:** How about joining the football club?

   Dan and Lisa: Why not? We _____. (love)

4 **Brian:** Why don't you try out for the basketball team?

   Dan and Lisa: Definitely not! We _____. (enjoy)

1 Complete the sentences. Use the correct form of the verbs in brackets.

1
My parents _____ (get married) when they _____ (be) very young. A few months later, they _____ (move) to London.

2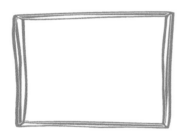
My father _____ (open) his own restaurant in Brighton when I _____ (be) a teenager. I _____ (work) with my father every weekend. A few years ago, I _____ (help) my father open his second restaurant.

2 Read and draw the pictures. Then write the answers.

1 Alice is shorter than Carl. Barbara is taller than Alice but shorter than Carl.

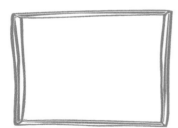

Who's the tallest?

_____

2 Jose is younger than Frank. Frank is older than Edward. Edward is older than Jose.

Who's the youngest?

_____

3 My brother, Ted, is very strong. He's stronger than my dad. My dad is stronger than my mum. I'm Mark. I'm stronger than Ted.

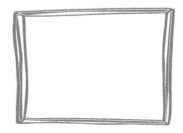

Who's the strongest in the family?

_____

1 How could pupils help their school? Make suggestions. Use could and the words from the box.

> clean up the playground   paint the art room   plant trees

1 Sophia   _____
   _____

2 Brian   _____
   _____

3 Jilly   _____
   _____

2 Unscramble the words. Then write sentences with am/is/are going to. What are these pupils going to do this week?

1 shaw arsc   We _____.

_____

2 rweti alteircs   Peter and Jake _____.

_____

3 abek sceak   I _____.

_____

4 eakm sptrseo   Rebecca _____.

_____

1 Look at the chart. Complete the sentences. Use more/less … than or the least/the most and the words in brackets.

	Jeff	Tony	Silvia
Making a volcano	👍👍	👍👍	👍
Mixing liquids	👍	👍	👍👍
Making electricity	👍👍👍	👍👍	👍👍👍

How did the pupils feel about their science class experiments?

1 **Silvia:** Mixing liquids was _____ making a volcano. (interesting)

2 **Jeff:** Making electricity was _____ of all. (exciting)

3 **Tony:** Mixing liquids was _____ experiment. (amazing)

4 **Jeff:** Making a volcano was _____ making electricity. (challenging)

2 Look at 1. Write sentences. Use as … as or not as … as.

1 **Jeff:** Making a volcano / fun / making electricity.

_____

2 **Tony:** Making electricity / exciting / making a volcano.

_____

3 **Silvia:** Mixing liquids / interesting / making electricity.

_____

3 Look at 1. Write sentences. Use too or not enough and the words in brackets.

1 **Silvia:** I didn't like making a volcano. It was _____. (interesting)

2 **Jeff:** Mixing liquids wasn't fun. It was _____. (boring)

3 **Tony:** I'm not interested in mixing liquids. It was _____. (exciting)

1 Match the puzzle pieces. Then complete the story. Use the sentences on the puzzle pieces and the correct form of the verbs.

Charlie's Silly Dream

his Maths book / sing him songs

She / turn the pancakes

Charlie / fall asleep

Charlie / walk to school

Charlie / have a snack

his backpack / began to fly

The bananas / jog on the table

the pancakes / start dancing

In the morning

Charlie's mother was making pancakes for breakfast.

1 _____ when _____ .

"Time for school, Charlie," said his mum.

2 _____ when _____ .

In the afternoon

Charlie was hungry.

3 _____ while _____ .

At night

Charlie was doing his Maths homework. Then he got very tired.

4 _____ while _____ .

His football turned off the light. "Goodnight, Charlie."

2 Circle the correct answers.

1 What was Charlie doing when his backpack began to fly?

  a He was walking to school.   **b** He walked to school.

2 What was his mum doing when the pancakes started dancing?

  a She was making breakfast.   **b** She made breakfast.

3 Was Charlie jogging when he had a snack?

  a No, he didn't.   **b** No, he wasn't.

4 Was he sleeping when the football turned out the light?

  a Yes, he was.   **b** Yes, he did.

1 Read. Then complete the sentences. Use no one and everyone.

One hundred years
from now...

100 years from now, the world will be very different. ¹_____ will use smartphones because our phones will be inside our heads!
²_____ will use flying cars and ³_____ will live in flats in tall buildings in space. Not like today. Today, many people live in houses. In the future, ⁴_____ will live in houses any more. Machines will make our food at home and in restaurants. ⁵_____ will need to cook any more. ⁶_____ will study in schools because there won't be any school buildings and we won't have teachers. ⁷_____ will study at home using computers.

2 Look at 1. Complete the sentences. Use will or won't and the verbs in brackets.

1 There _____ any teachers. (be)

2 We _____ people with mobile phones. (call)

3 We _____ in flats in space. (live)

4 People _____ flying cars. (drive)

5 We _____. (cook) Machines _____ (cook)
   for us.

3 Match the sentences. Write the letters.

In the future...

___ 1 Pupils won't need teachers.   **a** We'll meet by video messaging.

___ 2 We'll go to the moon on holiday.   **b** They'll teach themselves.

___ 3 No one will go to friends' houses.   **c** Nobody will be sad.

___ 4 Everyone will be happy.   **d** Spaceship travel will be cheap.

4 Look at 3. Do you think these things will happen? Write your answers.

_____

_____

_____

1 Complete the sentences. Use is/are used to and the words from the box.

> eat   get around   protect eyes   write

1 A pencil _____.

2 Plates _____.

3 A bike _____.

4 Sunglasses _____.

2 What do you think these things are? Write sentences. Use It may be or It might be.

1

_____

2

_____

3

_____

4

_____

3 Answer the questions. Use the words in brackets.

1 I'm thinking of something. It's round and it bounces. People play a game with it. What do you think it is?

_____ (may)

2 I'm thinking of a type of sweet food. They're small and taste nice. They're often seen at birthday parties. What do you think they are?

_____ (might)

3 I'm thinking of a small insect. It likes hot, wet weather. It can fly and it makes a noise when it flies. What do you think it is?

_____ (might)

1 Complete the sentences. Use the correct passive form of the verb in brackets.

1 The very first biscuit _____ in about the 7th century in Persia. (invent)

2 Crops, such as rice and wheat, _____ in many countries today. (grow)

3 In 2005, a bowl of noodles four thousand years old _____ by scientists in China. (discover)

4 Bananas _____ in the Caribbean every year. (pick)

5 A lot of coffee _____ in Colombia these days. (produce)

2 Complete the puzzle. Write the letters. Use the words from the box.

Africa	Argentina	Brazil	China
invent	mine	produce	raise

1	2	3	4
A __ __ m __ **d i a m o n d s** __ __ __	A __ __ r __ **c a t t l e** __ __ __ __ __ __	C __ __ __ i __ **n o o d l e s** __ __	B p **r u b b e r** __ __ __ __ __ __

3 Look at 2. Write sentences. Use is/are or was/were and the words in the puzzle.

1 _____

2 _____

3 _____

4 _____

1 Look at the chart. Complete and answer the questions.

	fly to the UK	win a spelling quiz	ride a horse	visit China	eat octopus
Georgina	✓			✓	✓
Rob		✓	✓		✓

1 _____ Georgina ever _____ to the UK?

_____

2 _____ Georgina ever _____ a spelling quiz?

_____

3 _____ Georgina ever _____ China?

_____

Georgina

4 _____ Rob ever _____ octopus?

_____

5 _____ Rob ever _____ a horse?

_____

Rob

2 Read. Then complete and answer the questions.

> Tom and Sara like spicy food, adventurous sports, beaches and adrenalin rushes.
> Karen likes unusual food but she doesn't like hot spices, scary sports, mountains
> or adrenalin rushes.

1 _____ Karen _____ eat spicy food or an avocado dessert?

_____

2 _____ Tom and Sara _____ visit a museum or ski down
a mountain?

_____

3 _____ Sara _____ go swimming or mountain climbing?

_____

4 _____ Tom and Sara _____ ride a motorcycle fast or slowly?

_____

5 _____ Karen _____ ski fast down a mountain or walk in
the woods?

_____

Young Learners English Practice
Flyers

Note to pupils:

These practice materials will help you prepare
for the YLE (Young Learners English) Tests.
There are three kinds of practice materials in this sampler:
Listening, Reading & Writing and Speaking.
Good luck!

Young Learner's English Practice Flyers: Listening A

– 5 questions –

 Listen and draw lines. There is one example.

Peter   Michael   Robert   Emma

Richard   David   Katy

– 5 questions –

 Listen and write. There is one example.

Greenfields Camp

Where: _in the Peak District_

1 **Activities:** _____

2 **How long:** _____

3 **Cost:** _____

4 **When the next camp begins:** _____

5 **What to bring:** _____

Young Learner's English Practice Flyers: Listening C

– 5 questions –

 What do the Martins and the Browns like to do?

Listen and write a letter in each box. There is one example.

 **Mrs Martin**

 **Mr Brown** ☐

 **Kelly Martin** ☐

 **David Martin** ☐

 **John Brown** ☐

 **Cindy Brown** ☐

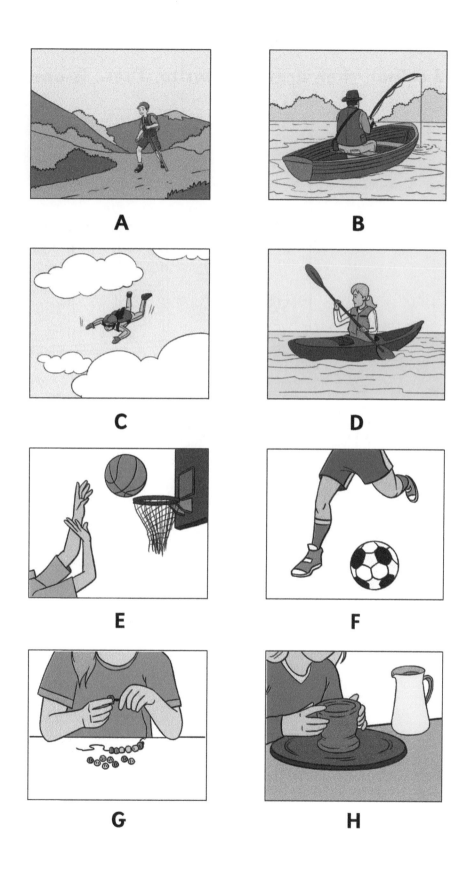

A

B

C

D

E

F

G

H

Young Learner's English Practice Flyers: Listening D

– 5 questions –

 Listen and colour, then draw and write. There is one example.

Young Learner's English Practice Flyers: Reading & Writing A

– 10 questions –

Look and read. Choose the correct words and write them on the lines. There is one example.

aunt   delicious   bracelet   graduate

school orchestra

insect repellent

silver

drama club

expensive

a kayak

an article   cake sale   a smartphone

She's your father's sister. _____aunt_____

1 This group puts on plays. If you're an actor, you should try it! _____

2 If you're a musician and know how to play an instrument, this is the group for you. _____

3 You'll do this when you finish university. _____

4 You could write this to tell people about something your school club is doing to raise money. _____

5 Earrings or necklaces are often made of this. _____

6 When something tastes really nice, this is how it tastes. _____

7 Take this with you when you go hiking so mosquitoes won't bite you. _____

8 You can use this to listen to music, play games or call someone. _____

9 You can ride in this kind of boat. It only fits one or two people. _____

10 We use this word to talk about something that costs a lot of money. _____

Young Learner's English Practice Flyers: Reading & Writing B

– 6 questions –

Read the story. Choose a word from the box. Write the correct word next to numbers 1–5. There is one example.

Mark and his classmates entered a contest at a science fair. The contest was to see which team could create the most useful ___invention___. Mark's team created a (1) _____ that could clean an entire house. It could clean the living room (2) _____, too. The judges were impressed but the other team also had a good idea. They showed off an (3) _____ that could store over 5,000 songs. Probably the most interesting thing about it was its source of power. It didn't use a (4) _____. It was (5) _____. The problem was you had to leave it in the sun every day for three hours. The judges didn't think that was practical so Mark and his team won.

Example

invention	battery	speakers	spaceship	solar-powered
mp3 player	robot	laptop	radio	furniture

(6) Now choose the best name for the story.

Tick (✓) one box.

Inventions Through History ☐

Two Heads Are Better Than One ☐

A Winning Idea ☐

Young Learner's English Practice Flyers: Reading & Writing C

– 8 questions –

Read the text. Choose the correct words and write them on the lines.

Costa Rica – Land of Adventure!

Example	Costa Rica is a country in Central America.
	Costa Rica is ___Known___ for its many beautiful
1	beaches, mountains and forests. It is _____
	by millions of people every year. People go to
2	Costa Rica _____ see amazing animals
	and to be close to nature. But there are many
3	_____ activities in Costa Rica, too. Have
4	you _____ heard of ziplining?
5	A zipline is a long wire. It's _____ of metal.
6	A zipline is used _____ travelling from one
	place to another, high above the ground. You can
7	ride on a zipline in the forest _____ go
8	from tree to tree. Are you _____? Maybe
	ziplining is for you!

Example	know	knew	known
1	visit	visiting	visited
2	in	for	to
3	unusual	spicy	delicious
4	done	ever	had
5	did	made	invent
6	to	then	for
7	doing	for	to
8	terrible	different	adventurous

Young Learner's English Practice Flyers: Speaking A

Find the differences

Candidate's copy

Out to dinner with Emma's family

What kind / restaurant	?
What / having	?
What / made of	?
What / taste like	?
Emma / ever tried	?

Information exchange

Out to dinner with Michael's family

What kind / restaurant	Chinese
What / having	hot and sour soup
What / made of	broth and vegetables
What / taste like	delicious
Michael / ever tried	yes

1   A: Hi, Jacob. Are you free this Saturday?

1   A: Guess what, Amanda. I'm moving.

A: Oh, yes? Where does your uncle live?

A: I know. We lived there when I was five.

A: My dad's got a new job in London.

A: Me too. Oh, I could lend you my mini DVD player.

A: Yes, we do. I know… how about having a party before I move?

B: Really? That'd be great! I could watch a few films. Thanks.

B: You are? But you just moved here two years ago! Why are you moving?

B: Oh, I see. London, hmm. That's a big city.

B: That sounds like fun. We could invite some of our friends.

B: No, I'm not. My Uncle Steven is getting married this weekend. We're going to drive there on Saturday morning.

B: You did? Wow. Your family moves a lot.

B: He lives about four hours away from here by car. I hate sitting in the car that long.

was camping

I got a lot of mosquito bites.

was cycling

I fell and hurt my leg.

was walking on the beach

I got sunburnt.

was playing football in the park

I lost my house keys.

was playing basketball outside

I suddenly felt hungry.

was taking the dog for a walk

It started to rain.

write a short story

write an apology email for something you did wrong

ride a rollercoaster by yourself

ride on a merry-go-round with all your friends

be a performer in a talent show

be a contestant on a TV game show

go to an opera

go to a chess tournament

eat a chocolate-covered insect

eat ice cream with chilli peppers

get the highest mark in your class in a Maths test

get the highest score in your neighbourhood on a video game